Culture of Excellence

Success Starts with Culture

Unleashing Leadership Excellence Series:

Book 1 - Clear and Confident: The Communication Playbook

Book 2 - Culture of Excellence: Success Starts with Culture

Book 3 - Resolving Conflicts with Confidence:
    Empowering Your Approach to Conflict

Copyright © 2024 Timothy K Ellsworth

All rights reserved

The characters and events portrayed in this book are fictitious. Any similarity to real persons, living or dead, is coincidental and not intended by the author.

No part of this book may be reproduced, or stored in a retrieval system, or transmitted in any form or by any means, electronic, mechanical, photocopying, recording, or otherwise, without express written permission of the publisher.

ISBN: 9798340960474

CONTENTS

Copyright
Introduction
Values to Victory — 1
Cultivating Unity — 6
Clear Communication. — 14
Together Triumph — 21
The Power of Us — 28
Where Trust Leads — 35
The Praise Effect — 43
Cultivating Connections — 51
Stronger Bonds — 61
Emotional Intelligence — 77
Walking the Talk — 91
Culture Killers — 101
Conclusion — 114

Foreword

With nearly three decades of unwavering dedication to the logistics industry, I invite you to join me on a transformative journey toward building a strong, empowering work culture. My professional story began on the floor as a machine operator, and over the years, it has evolved into a deep exploration of how to unlock the hidden potential within individuals and organizations by fostering a culture that truly engages and inspires. Throughout my varied career, I have taken on many roles, mentor, coach, trainer, and each experience has enriched my understanding of the profound impact that a positive, inclusive work culture can have on a team. The insights I have gained have shaped my approach to leadership and highlighted the essential role that culture plays in driving team engagement, motivation, and overall success. Today, I am excited to share these insights with you in this comprehensive guide, The Culture of Excellence. This guide is the culmination of years spent refining principles of leadership and culture-building, drawing from my personal journey and the lessons learned from the many mentors and mentees who have been part of my career. It is designed as a practical resource for leaders who are committed to creating and sustaining a work culture where every team member feels valued, motivated, and fully engaged. At the heart of this guide is the belief that true success in leadership comes from cultivating an environment where team members are empowered to thrive. When leaders focus on building a strong culture, one that prioritizes trust, inclusivity, and mutual respect, they unlock the full potential of their teams, leading to greater collaboration, innovation, and overall achievement. I invite you to embark on this journey with me as we explore strategies for building a work culture that not only supports individual growth but also strengthens the team as a whole. Whether you are a seasoned executive seeking to enhance your organization's culture or an emerging leader eager to make a positive impact, The Culture of Excellence is crafted to empower you with the knowledge and tools needed to create a thriving, engaged workforce.

Join me as we dive into the transformative power of culture, where a commitment to building strong, positive relationships serves as the foundation for unparalleled success. Welcome to your guide to creating a work environment where every team member is empowered to contribute their best.

Warm regards,

Timothy Ellsworth

INTRODUCTION

The true measure of a high-performing team lies not only in productivity but in the unity, motivation, and resilience of its members. Building such a team requires more than just technical expertise and hard work; it demands a deliberate effort to cultivate a culture that aligns with shared values, promotes inclusivity, encourages transparency, and celebrates collective victories. This culture serves as the foundation upon which excellence is built, creating an environment where every team member feels valued, supported, and empowered to contribute their best. As we embark on this journey of understanding what it takes to build and sustain a thriving team, we will explore the key elements that make a significant impact on team dynamics. From establishing a culture of excellence rooted in shared values to fostering an environment of transparency and open communication, each chapter of this book will guide you through the essential steps needed to transform your team into a cohesive and unstoppable force. We will dive into the importance of collaboration, the role of trust, the power of recognition, and the ways to cultivate lasting connections within your team. These components are not just complementary but are deeply interconnected, forming the bedrock of a culture that drives success. Whether you are a leader aiming to inspire your team or a team member striving to contribute to a positive work environment, the insights and strategies presented here will equip you with the tools needed to create a team culture where everyone thrives. Together, we will explore how to move from values to victory, from collaboration to triumph, and ultimately, from a group of individuals to a unified team that achieves greatness.

VALUES TO VICTORY
The Path to Excellence.

Building a strong work culture begins with establishing core values that serve as the cornerstone of everything your team does. These values are not just abstract ideas; they form the foundation of a cohesive, supportive, and high-performing environment. When deeply integrated into daily operations, these values guide behaviour, decision-making, and interactions, ensuring that every team member contributes to a unified and purpose-driven workplace. In this chapter, we will explore the critical steps necessary to establish these core values and embed them into the fabric of your organization. We'll discuss how to identify values that truly resonate with your team, engage them in the process to foster ownership, and seamlessly integrate these values into everyday work life. By the end of this chapter, you will have a solid framework for creating a value-driven culture that supports and propels your team towards collective success. Identifying the core values that will become the cornerstone of your work culture is the first and most crucial step in this process. These values are not merely conceptual; they are the fundamental principles that will define how your team operates, interacts, and grows together. To establish a workplace where every team member feels connected, valued, and motivated, these core values must embody the essence of what it means to be part of your team, a part of your organization. Trust is often the cornerstone of any robust work culture. In your workplace, trust extends beyond simply relying on colleagues to fulfill their roles; it encompasses a belief in each other's integrity, capabilities, and intentions. Trust fosters an environment where team members feel safe to express their thoughts, take risks, and support each other without fear of judgment or reprisal. This level of trust is essential for open communication and collaboration, allowing the team to function with a unity that is difficult to achieve otherwise. Establishing trust requires consistent actions and transparent communication. As a leader, you must model trustworthy behaviour, keep your promises, be honest about challenges, and show vulnerability when necessary. This sets the tone for the entire team, encouraging everyone to act with integrity and dependability. Respect is another crucial value that works hand in hand with trust. In a work environment that values respect, all team member's contributions are acknowledged and valued, regardless of their role or background. Respect is about creating a space where everyone's voice is heard, differences are celebrated rather than marginalized, and mutual understanding is prioritized. A culture of respect is demonstrated through active listening, thoughtful communication, and a willingness to consider perspectives that differ from one's own. When respect is deeply ingrained in your work culture, it minimizes conflicts, enhances teamwork, and fosters a sense of belonging among all team members. It creates an environment where individuals are treated with dignity, their ideas are given due consideration, and their efforts are recognized and appreciated. Support within the team is another vital component of a strong work culture. In a supportive environment, team members are more than just coworkers; they are allies who can rely on one another through challenges and successes alike. Support manifests in various ways, from offering help on a difficult project to providing emotional encouragement during stressful times. A culture of support ensures that no one feels isolated or overwhelmed; instead, team members know they can count on each other for assistance and understanding. This mutual support strengthens the bonds within the team, leading to higher morale, greater job satisfaction, and a more resilient organization overall. As a leader, fostering this supportive atmosphere requires actively checking in on your team members, offering help when needed, and encouraging a spirit of camaraderie and cooperation. Collaboration is a value that must be prioritized over competition within your work culture. In many workplaces, competition can lead to a cutthroat atmosphere where individual success is valued more than collective achievement. However, in a culture that values collaboration, the focus shifts to working together to achieve common goals. Collaboration encourages sharing knowledge, resources, and ideas, fostering innovation and problem-solving that benefit the entire team. When collaboration is a core value, it reduces silos and promotes a more inclusive, team-oriented approach to work. This shift from "me" to "we" ensures that successes are shared, and challenges are faced together, creating a stronger, more united team. Building a strong work culture starts with deliberate actions to cultivate trust, respect, support, and collaboration, but achieving these ideals requires a nuanced approach. Trust, for instance, is not built overnight, it is nurtured through consistent, authentic actions over time. Leaders must prioritize creating an environment where transparency thrives, and accountability is embraced at every level. Trust grows stronger in organizations where both leaders and team members demonstrate reliability, own their mistakes, and share both successes and challenges openly. Respect forms the bedrock of healthy interpersonal interactions within the workplace. It's reflected not only in how people communicate but also in how they listen and engage with one another. Beyond superficial gestures, respect must be deeply ingrained in the team's culture, manifesting in deliberate practices like acknowledging diverse viewpoints, offering constructive feedback, and addressing conflicts with empathy and professionalism. When team members feel their voices are heard and their perspectives valued, they are empowered to bring their best selves to the organization. Support within the team serves as a safety net that catches individuals during moments of challenge. This goes beyond professional aid; emotional support creates an atmosphere of psychological safety, which fosters creativity and risk-taking. Leaders should actively create moments of connection through team-building activities or informal check-ins that deepen bonds and reinforce the message that every team member is valued, not just for what they produce but for who they are. Collaboration is perhaps the glue that binds all other core values into actionable synergy. A truly collaborative workplace rejects isolationism and thrives on the collective intelligence of its members. Encouraging open dialogue, brainstorming sessions, and cross-functional projects can dismantle silos and pave the way for innovations that arise from collective input. Leaders should exemplify this by promoting the idea that shared knowledge is power. Accountability complements collaboration by establishing a culture where team members take responsibility for their roles while relying on each other's contributions. In organizations with accountability as a core value, team members can trust that everyone is dedicated to achieving common goals without unnecessary finger-pointing or blame. This strengthens morale and assures everyone that they are contributing to meaningful progress. Integrity underscores every interaction in a value-driven organization, ensuring consistency between what the team says and does. When leaders model ethical behaviour and demonstrate unwavering fairness, it sets an example for all. This adherence to ethical standards minimizes instances of hypocrisy or favoritism, thereby boosting morale and alignment with the team's overarching mission. Inclusivity ensures that the organization remains a space where diverse talents and perspectives are welcomed and nurtured. The workplace must actively cultivate an environment where barriers are dismantled, whether they are rooted in biases, structural challenges, or limited opportunities for certain groups. By celebrating uniqueness, the organization enriches its culture and drives meaningful growth. Continuous learning rounds out the key components of a vibrant work culture. Creating opportunities for professional growth, encouraging curiosity, and rewarding innovation positions the organization as not just a workplace but a space for personal and collective transformation. Teams must be encouraged to view every challenge as a chance to learn and improve, which fosters resilience and long-term success. Recognition and celebration play an often-underappreciated role in embedding values into a work culture. Frequent acknowledgment of contributions, whether big or small, fosters a positive feedback loop that encourages alignment with core values. Milestones, achievements, and even day-to-day efforts should be celebrated as they reflect the underlying principles of the organization. Adaptability ensures the sustainability of your core values in an ever-changing world. By fostering a mindset that embraces change, the organization can consistently uphold its values while responding to new challenges and opportunities. Leaders and teams must be willing to reassess and evolve their practices without compromising their foundational beliefs, ensuring longevity and relevance. Once you have identified these core values, trust, respect, support, and collaboration, it's time to ensure they are deeply embedded into your team's daily operations. This process involves more than just setting down a list of ideals; it requires engaging your team in meaningful discussions and collaborative decision-making to create values that everyone can stand behind. By actively involving your team in defining these values, you foster a sense of ownership and commitment, ensuring that the values are not just words on paper but are lived and breathed every day. To ensure that these values resonate deeply within your organization, it's essential to involve your team in defining them. When team members actively contribute to the creation of these values, they are more likely to take ownership and consistently uphold them in their daily interactions. This sense of ownership fosters a stronger commitment to the values and ensures they are more than just words on a page, they become integral to the team's identity and operations. Effective communication is key to embedding these values into your team's culture. Once the core values are defined, the next crucial step is to communicate them clearly and effectively across the organization. It's vital that these values are not merely words on a wall but are actively lived and breathed by every member of the team. This communication ensures that the values permeate all levels of the organization, becoming a fundamental part of the daily work experience and guiding behaviours and decisions. As you establish your work values as the cornerstone of your culture, remember that this is an ongoing process. The values must be regularly revisited, reinforced, and integrated into all aspects of your organization. By embedding these values into the fabric of your daily operations, you create a workplace where every team member feels connected, valued, and committed to a shared purpose, a place where your work values truly guide the culture.

CULTURE OF EXELLENCE

CULTIVATING UNITY
The Journey to Inclusion.

Creating a sense of belonging within a team is a foundational strategy that drives both individual fulfillment and organizational success. When team members feel truly included, valued, and integral to the group, they become more engaged, motivated, and committed to their work. This sense of belonging transforms a collection of individuals into a cohesive, collaborative, and high-performing team. In such an environment, creativity flourishes, productivity rises, and retention rates improve. Belonging not only enhances job satisfaction but also reduces workplace stress, leading to a more resilient and adaptable team. In this chapter, we will dive into the steps necessary to cultivate a powerful sense of belonging within your team. We will discuss the importance of implementing inclusive practices, encouraging meaningful personal connections, celebrating diversity, and establishing robust feedback mechanisms. Each of these elements plays a vital role in constructing a workplace where every team member feels they belong, contributing to a unified and strong team culture. Additionally, it is crucial to recognize the subtle ways in which favouritism can undermine these efforts. While the focus of this chapter is on building unity, it's important to remain aware of the impact of favouritism, consciously avoiding it to ensure that all team members feel equally valued. Inclusivity is the bedrock of belonging. It's not enough to have a diverse team; inclusivity ensures that every individual, regardless of their background or position, feels respected and integral to the team's success. Achieving true inclusivity requires more than surface-level efforts; it demands a deep commitment to creating an environment where all voices are heard, all contributions are valued, and every individual has a stake in the collective success of the team. One of the first steps in fostering inclusivity is creating opportunities for every team member to contribute meaningfully to discussions and decision-making processes. This involves moving beyond traditional top-down communication structures and establishing a culture of open communication where input from all levels of the organization is actively sought. Regular team meetings are essential platforms for this, but they should be structured to encourage participation from everyone. Consider rotating the responsibility of leading meetings among team members, which can empower quieter voices and ensure different perspectives are heard. Inclusivity also requires leaders to be proactive in addressing the power dynamics that can silence certain voices. This might involve setting ground rules for meetings that ensure respectful dialogue and equal airtime for all participants. By creating multiple channels for feedback and communication, you can ensure that everyone feels they have a voice in the team's direction and decisions. It's also important to be mindful of the way tasks and opportunities are distributed within the team. Are certain individuals consistently given more high-visibility projects, while others are relegated to less important tasks? If so, consider how this distribution might impact team morale and the perception of fairness. Leaders should strive to distribute opportunities equitably, using strategies like cross-training and mentoring to ensure all team members have the chance to develop and shine. This approach not only fosters a sense of fairness but also reinforces the idea that all contributions are essential to the team's success. While it's natural to have different relationships with team members, it's crucial to avoid favouritism or the appearance of it, as this can quickly erode trust and unity within the team. Personal connections within the team are equally important in building a sense of belonging. When team members develop relationships that go beyond their professional roles, it fosters a sense of trust and mutual respect that is essential for a cohesive team culture. These personal connections transform a group of colleagues into a community where individuals feel genuinely cared for and supported. One of the most effective ways to encourage personal connections is through team-building activities that allow members to interact in a more relaxed, informal setting. These activities should be designed to help team members get to know each other on a personal level, beyond their work roles. However, not all team members will feel comfortable in the same social settings. Some may be introverted or have personal reasons for not wanting to participate in group activities. As a leader, it's crucial to offer a variety of opportunities for personal connections, catering to different personalities and preferences. This could include smaller, more intimate gatherings, one-on-one coffee chats, or virtual meetups for remote team members. The goal is to create multiple avenues for team members to connect in ways that feel authentic and comfortable for them, without pressuring anyone to participate in activities that don't align with their comfort level. Celebrating personal milestones and achievements is another powerful way to foster personal connections. Whether it's a birthday, a work anniversary, or a personal achievement outside of work, these moments provide opportunities to show that the team cares about the individual beyond their professional contributions. Recognizing these events can be as simple as acknowledging them in a team meeting or sending a congratulatory message. These gestures contribute to a work environment where individuals feel valued as whole people, not just as employees. Importantly, when celebrating achievements, it's vital to ensure that all team members receive recognition fairly, which helps avoid any perception of favouritism. Diversity is not just a checkbox to be ticked; it is a vital source of strength, creativity, and innovation within a team. Celebrating diversity means recognizing and honoring the unique backgrounds, experiences, and perspectives that each team member brings to the table. This celebration is crucial for creating a work environment where everyone feels seen, respected, and valued for who they are, not just for what they do. One of the most powerful ways to celebrate diversity is by creating opportunities for team members to share their stories and cultural traditions with the group. This could be done through organized cultural events, where team members are invited to share aspects of their heritage, such as traditional foods, music, or customs. In addition to cultural celebrations, it's important to encourage discussions around diversity and inclusion within the team. These discussions should be open, respectful, and aimed at increasing understanding and empathy among team members. Leaders can facilitate these conversations by creating spaces where team members feel comfortable sharing their experiences and perspectives on diversity-related issues. It's also important to be proactive in addressing any incidents of bias or discrimination that may arise, ensuring that the workplace remains a safe and welcoming environment for all. The process of creating a sense of belonging begins the moment a new team member walks through the door, making the on-boarding process a critical touchpoint. A welcoming and inclusive onboarding experience sets the tone for how new hires will perceive their place within the team. It's essential to go beyond the standard introduction to job responsibilities and focus on integrating new employees into the team culture from the outset. A successful onboarding process should begin with clear communication about the team's values, expectations, and culture. New hires need to understand not just what is expected of them in terms of their work but also how they can contribute to and thrive within the team's cultural environment. Assigning mentors or buddies is another essential component of a welcoming onboarding experience. A mentor or buddy can serve as a guide for the new hire, helping them navigate both the formal aspects of their new role and the informal dynamics of the team. This person can answer questions, provide advice, and introduce the new hire to other team members, making the transition smoother and less intimidating. Involving the new hire in team activities and projects early on is also crucial. This immediate engagement helps them understand their role within the team and start building relationships with their colleagues. Leaders should ensure that new employees receive regular feedback during their initial period, which helps them adjust and feel confident in their contributions. Feedback is a critical tool for fostering a sense of belonging and ensuring that it endures over time. Establishing robust feedback mechanisms allows team members to express their thoughts, experiences, and suggestions, providing leaders with valuable insights into how well the team's culture is being upheld and where improvements might be needed. By actively seeking and responding to feedback, leaders demonstrate their commitment to creating a work environment where everyone feels heard, valued, and included. To be effective, feedback mechanisms must be diverse and accessible. One-on-one meetings between team members and their supervisors offer a personalized space for open and honest dialogue. Anonymous surveys can also be valuable, particularly for gathering input from those who may be hesitant to speak up in person. In addition to formal feedback mechanisms, leaders should cultivate a culture of continuous, informal feedback. This can be encouraged through open-door policies, where team members feel comfortable approaching their supervisors at any time with concerns or suggestions.

Regular team meetings can also be used as opportunities to discuss the team's culture and brainstorm ways to enhance inclusivity and belonging. Feedback should be viewed not as a one-time event but as a continuous process. Regularly scheduled feedback sessions, ongoing surveys, and a culture that encourages open communication all contribute to a dynamic and responsive work environment. Building a culture of belonging requires consistent, intentional engagement with every team member, emphasizing the human connection beyond work roles. It begins by demonstrating genuine interest in who they are as individuals, not just what they contribute professionally. This includes creating opportunities for team members to share their stories, celebrate their passions, and bring their unique perspectives to the forefront. By fostering open communication, you invite vulnerability, understanding, and empathy into the workspace. This simple act of recognition helps bridge gaps, minimize misunderstandings, and cultivate trust that solidifies the foundation of your team culture. Inclusivity is strengthened through a leader's active effort to establish equitable opportunities and eliminate hidden biases. Start by assessing existing team dynamics and policies to uncover areas where inclusivity might be unintentionally stifled. Evaluate decision-making processes, workload distribution, and leadership practices to ensure they align with the values of fairness and diversity. By openly inviting suggestions for improvement, you show humility and model the adaptability needed for progress. This introspective work is as much about educating yourself as it is about creating meaningful systemic changes that amplify every voice. Belonging requires collaboration across all hierarchical levels, transforming the way decisions are made and work is executed. Rather than imposing solutions, embrace participatory leadership. Solicit input and engage in shared problem-solving, allowing the collective wisdom of the team to shine. Encourage your team to challenge assumptions respectfully, propose ideas, and co-create strategies that align with shared goals. Collaboration in action reflects the inclusivity that anchors belonging, it's not only empowering but ensures the success of initiatives born from diverse insights. Creating psychological safety plays a significant role in building belonging. Every team member must feel safe to express their concerns, share their ideas, and admit their mistakes without fear of criticism or retribution. Openly acknowledge your own challenges and areas of growth to normalize the imperfections inherent in everyone. Offer reassurance through consistent, patient responses to feedback and mistakes. This intentional atmosphere of grace paves the way for mutual respect and contributes to personal growth while fostering a more innovative and cohesive team environment. Empowerment is an often-overlooked component of belonging. Equip team members with the tools, resources, and confidence they need to excel in their roles. Share constructive, strengths-based feedback regularly and offer personalized development opportunities that build on each individual's unique potential. Providing empowerment in this manner leads to heightened engagement, improved morale, and an energized work culture where people feel valued for both their contributions and their growth trajectories. Transparency strengthens trust and contributes to feelings of inclusion and fairness. Leaders must model honesty and open communication while addressing sensitive topics, from strategic shifts to mistakes that impact the group. Transparency is not synonymous with oversharing, it's about informing your team with the appropriate balance of candor and tact, allowing them to participate in or understand decision-making processes. This openness instills a collective sense of ownership in your shared vision. Building resilience is integral to a sense of belonging because resilience allows teams to bounce back together after challenges. Celebrate perseverance and the lessons that emerge during tough times. When a project or task doesn't unfold as anticipated, gather your team to reflect on successes within the setback. Turn disappointment into shared insight by ensuring individuals feel supported, not blamed. This approach fosters trust, reduces stress, and reinforces belonging, even in the face of difficulty. Recognizing individuality while maintaining collective alignment requires a delicate balance. Strive to celebrate what makes each person unique while connecting their passions to the team's objectives. For example, tailor roles or projects to suit distinctive talents. Frame your recognition of their individuality as essential to the team's broader mission. When individuality is linked with organizational success, it cultivates pride and reinforces the belief that every person matters profoundly. Encourage the celebration of achievements and contributions without competitive undercurrents. Shift the focus from "best performer" comparisons to "team victories" while highlighting each member's contributions. Incorporating a habit of celebrating smaller, everyday successes reinforces positive momentum. Simple gestures, such as sending personalized acknowledgements or recognizing contributions during meetings, significantly deepen bonds and convey gratitude. Address team dynamics proactively by managing interpersonal conflicts with fairness, empathy, and consistency. Empower team members with conflict-resolution strategies and intervene with clarity when personal issues hinder professional harmony. Foster a culture that doesn't avoid challenges but encourages constructive resolution. Your demonstration of steady and unbiased leadership through times of tension sets the standard for maintaining connection even under stress. Personal connections within the workplace often determine how deeply a sense of belonging is felt. As a leader, facilitate authentic relational interactions that allow your team members to see one another as real people rather than mere coworkers. Host monthly casual check-ins, create inclusive spaces for shared storytelling, or institute mentorship opportunities between veterans and newcomers. Over time, these personal connections humanize organizational goals and foster cohesion. Accessibility to leadership transforms hierarchical divides into collective strength. Make yourself available both in scheduled times and unscheduled interactions, allowing team members the reassurance that their leader is approachable and caring. When they know your "door is always open," they are more likely to seek advice, offer feedback, or seek counsel, actions that improve alignment and enhance your culture of inclusion.

Advocating for inclusivity involves concrete structural adjustments. Move from performative diversity initiatives to those entrenched in authentic organizational change. This may involve auditing hiring practices to root out systemic biases, redesigning employee pathways to advancement, or partnering with local diversity-focused groups for recruitment. Through such intentional structural commitment, belonging ceases to be an abstract principle and becomes a tangible reality. Provide a roadmap for professional and personal development as an essential piece of fostering growth. Build detailed career frameworks while customizing mentorship to each person's goals. Regularly re-examine these plans as a living document, ensuring your support evolves in parallel with their professional aspirations and personal triumphs. Helping them reach their best potential directly enriches your shared mission. Normalize seeking and receiving constructive feedback as part of the work culture. When critique and growth-related conversations are depersonalized, individuals more readily engage in self-improvement. Train yourself and other leaders to embrace curiosity during performance reviews or conflicts. Shift from punitive language to constructive discussions focused on the shared investment in the success of the whole. Cultivating celebration with inclusivity in mind reduces unintended exclusion in group-based recognition events. Regularly evaluate how gatherings and award ceremonies are designed and received by all, not just the most vocal participants. Incorporate private moments of gratitude alongside public affirmations. These adjustments ensure no one feels invisible, even amid collaborative recognition. Strengthening collective vision keeps members invested beyond individual objectives. Start each fiscal cycle or quarter with sessions focused on understanding team alignment towards broader goals. Provide every participant context on how their role integrates into organizational impact. This macro-micro link sustains intrinsic motivation. Handling periods of change with clarity emphasizes to your team their value during uncertainty. Communicate how shifts in operations, staffing, or goals align with preserving core values of belonging. Directly addressing concerns alleviates anxiety while motivating continued shared purpose despite obstacles. Upholding traditions during high-intensity stretches, holidays or organizational crises, retains grounding amidst pressure. Maintain morale by prioritizing milestones such as shared breakfasts, thematic days, or gratitude cards during crunch seasons. Balanced energies across morale initiatives keep enthusiasm consistently distributed. Celebrate your entire journey collectively in concluding reflections across major team milestones. Prepare annual narratives that recount chapters containing authentic trials merged equally by gains. Bridging legacy artifacts within future commitments shows gratitude while rallying energy toward future initiatives beyond mere deliverable enumeration. Creating a sense of belonging within a team is a complex, ongoing process that requires deliberate effort, consistent action, and a deep commitment to inclusivity and connection. By fostering an inclusive environment where all voices are heard and valued, encouraging meaningful personal connections among team members, celebrating the diverse backgrounds and perspectives within the team, crafting a welcoming and comprehensive on-boarding experience, and establishing robust feedback mechanisms, you can build a work culture where every individual feels they belong. Throughout this journey, it is essential to be aware of favouritism, ensuring that all team members feel equally valued and included. This sense of belonging is not just beneficial for individual team members; it is the foundation of a high-performing, resilient, and cohesive team. When team members feel truly connected to one another and to the organization, they are more likely to contribute their best work, support their colleagues, and stay committed to the team's goals. This connection fuels a sense of shared purpose that transcends individual roles and responsibilities, aligning personal aspirations with collective objectives. When team members view themselves as integral to the organization's success, they not only perform tasks with greater diligence but also actively seek ways to improve processes, innovate solutions, and drive progress. A deeply connected team fosters a culture of mutual support and accountability. In such environments, colleagues are not just coworkers but trusted allies who understand and value each other's strengths and perspectives. This creates a network of encouragement and assistance that bolsters resilience during challenges and amplifies the celebration of achievements. As trust deepens, collaboration becomes second nature, and barriers like fear of judgment or hesitation to share ideas diminish. Commitment to the team's goals naturally becomes a byproduct of this connection. When individuals see their values reflected in their workplace and feel respected and appreciated, they are more likely to go above and beyond to ensure collective success. This kind of dedication inspires a domino effect, where one person's engagement uplifts others, resulting in an environment that not only achieves outcomes but surpasses expectations. By prioritizing connection, organizations set the stage for sustained growth, innovation, and long-term success.

CULTURE OF EXELLENCE

CLEAR COMMUNICATION.
Stronger Teams.

In any organization, communication is the lifeblood that connects every aspect of the team's work, relationships, and overall success. The ability to communicate openly and honestly is not just a skill, it's a cornerstone of a thriving organizational culture. When team members feel empowered to speak their minds without fear of judgment or reprisal, the result is a workplace characterized by trust, collaboration, and innovation. However, establishing and maintaining a culture where open communication is not only encouraged but also practiced consistently by all requires deliberate effort, thoughtful leadership, and a commitment to continuous improvement. The foundation of open communication begins with leadership. Leaders set the tone for how communication is perceived and practiced within the team. If leaders model transparency and approachability, it signals to everyone that open dialogue is valued and expected. This means that leaders must be willing to share information openly, even when it's difficult or uncomfortable. For example, when facing organizational challenges or changes, a transparent leader will provide clear and honest updates, explaining the situation, the rationale behind decisions, and the potential impact on the team. This openness fosters trust, as team members are more likely to feel included in the process and reassured by the honesty of their leaders. Being approachable is equally important. Leaders who are approachable create an environment where team members feel comfortable bringing up concerns, asking questions, or sharing ideas. This requires leaders to be physically and emotionally available, whether through an open-door policy, regular one-on-one meetings, or simply by making time to listen without distraction. An approachable leader demonstrates through their actions that they value what their team members have to say, and that they are open to feedback and dialogue. This sets the stage for a culture where open communication can flourish, as team members see that their voices will be heard and respected. Setting the tone is only the first step. To truly embed open communication into the fabric of the organization, it's essential to establish and maintain effective communication channels. These channels serve as the conduits through which information flows, ensuring that everyone is kept in the loop and that communication is not just top-down but multi-directional. Regular team meetings are one of the most effective ways to facilitate open communication. These meetings provide a structured space where the team can discuss ongoing projects, share updates, and address any challenges or concerns. It's important that these meetings are not solely focused on task completion but also on fostering dialogue and encouraging participation from all members. Leaders should make it a point to invite input, ask open-ended questions, and create an atmosphere where team members feel safe to speak up. In addition to team meetings, one-on-one sessions are crucial for deeper, more personal communication. These meetings allow for more focused discussions, where individuals can share their thoughts and concerns in a more private setting. It's during these sessions that leaders can build stronger relationships with their team members, understanding their unique perspectives, challenges, and aspirations. One-on-one meetings also provide an opportunity for leaders to give personalized feedback and support, further reinforcing the open communication culture. To maximize the effectiveness of these sessions, it's important that they are conducted regularly and with genuine interest in what the team member has to say. Digital tools also play a significant role in modern communication. With teams often spread across different locations, or even working remotely, having reliable and accessible digital communication platforms is essential. Tools like email, instant messaging, video conferencing, and project management software enable continuous communication, keeping everyone connected and informed. It's important to remember that digital communication, while convenient, can sometimes lead to misunderstandings or a lack of personal connection. Therefore, it's crucial to balance digital communication with face-to-face interactions, whether in-person or virtual, to maintain the personal touch that is often necessary for open and honest dialogue. Encouraging two-way dialogue is another critical aspect of building a culture of open communication. It's not enough for leaders to share information and expect it to be accepted without question; team members must also feel empowered to voice their thoughts, concerns, and ideas. This requires creating a culture where feedback is not only welcomed but actively sought out. Leaders can encourage this by regularly asking for input during meetings, conducting surveys to gather opinions on various issues, and fostering an environment where questioning and constructive criticism are seen as valuable contributions rather than challenges to authority. When team members see that their feedback is taken seriously and leads to tangible changes, they become more invested in the communication process and more likely to participate actively. To support two-way dialogue, it's essential to promote and train team members in active listening skills. Active listening is more than just hearing what someone else is saying; it involves fully engaging with the speaker, understanding their message, and responding thoughtfully. When team members practice active listening, they not only ensure that the speaker feels heard and understood, but they also contribute to a culture of respect and empathy within the team. Training in active listening can include workshops, role-playing exercises, or simply modeling these behaviours in everyday interactions. Encouraging team members to ask clarifying questions, repeat back what they've heard to confirm understanding, and respond without judgment are all key components of active listening that can greatly enhance communication. Despite the best efforts to foster open communication, barriers can still arise. These barriers may take many forms, from fear of reprisal or judgment to cultural differences that affect communication styles. Identifying and addressing these barriers is crucial for maintaining a culture of open and honest dialogue. One common barrier is the fear that speaking up might lead to negative consequences, such as being seen as a troublemaker or facing retaliation. To overcome this, leaders must make it clear that open communication is not only accepted but encouraged, and that there will be no negative repercussions for speaking the truth. This can be reinforced by recognizing and rewarding those who contribute openly, and by addressing any incidents where someone's voice may have been unfairly dismissed or penalized. Cultural differences can also create communication barriers, particularly in diverse teams where members may come from different backgrounds with varying communication norms. It's important for leaders to be aware of these differences and to foster an environment where all communication styles are respected. This might involve cultural sensitivity training, encouraging team members to share their communication preferences, or adapting communication strategies to accommodate different needs. By acknowledging and respecting these differences, leaders can create a more inclusive environment where everyone feels comfortable participating in open dialogue. Another potential barrier to open communication is the existence of cliques or subgroups within the team. When certain groups dominate the conversation, it can create an atmosphere where others feel excluded or hesitant to contribute. Leaders must be vigilant in recognizing and addressing these dynamics, ensuring that all team members have equal opportunities to speak and be heard. This might involve restructuring meetings to ensure more balanced participation, or actively encouraging quieter team members to share their thoughts. By breaking down these barriers, leaders can create a more cohesive and inclusive team where open communication thrives. It's important to recognize that open communication is not a one-time effort but an ongoing process that requires continuous reinforcement and adaptation. As the team evolves, so too must the communication strategies that support it. In the fabric of any organization, communication is the golden thread that weaves together the disparate elements of operations, culture, and collaboration. It is the difference between a team that merely functions and one that flourishes. Open communication fosters an environment where every team member feels like an integral part of the whole, contributing their unique perspectives without hesitation. This sense of belonging cultivates trust, trust in leadership, in the team, and in the mission. It's a trust that does not happen overnight but is built painstakingly through consistency, authenticity, and a genuine commitment to transparency. As this trust deepens, so does the capacity of the organization to innovate and adapt to challenges. To instill this sense of trust, leaders must first demonstrate vulnerability, a quality that is often overlooked yet undeniably powerful. When a leader admits to mistakes, acknowledges uncertainties, or seeks input on difficult decisions, it signals to the team that imperfection is a shared human experience and not a failing. This vulnerability humanizes leadership and breaks down barriers, making it easier for team members to voice their concerns or ask for help. This is especially important during times of change or uncertainty, where transparency from leadership can transform anxiety into assurance. Vulnerability fosters empathy, allowing connections to form on a deeper, more personal level. Beyond vulnerability, communication thrives on consistency. A team should never have to guess about where they stand or where the organization is headed. Regular updates, whether through meetings, emails, or informal check-ins, reinforce this sense of stability and predictability. This consistent flow of information empowers team members to align their efforts with the organization's goals and anticipate how their roles fit into the bigger picture. Importantly, consistency also applies to actions. When leaders act in accordance with their words, it sets the standard for integrity throughout the organization. Another pillar of open communication is fostering an environment that celebrates diverse voices and perspectives. When every team member, regardless of rank or background, feels that their contributions are valued, the team benefits from a wider range of ideas and solutions. This inclusivity begins with creating opportunities for participation, structured brainstorming sessions, open forums, or even informal discussions over coffee. But creating opportunities is just the starting point; leaders must actively seek out and encourage those who might otherwise hesitate to speak, ensuring that their voices are not only heard but welcomed. One of the most impactful practices for fostering open communication is active recognition. Acknowledging and appreciating the efforts and ideas of team members does more than boost morale, it reinforces the idea that their voices make a difference. Recognition doesn't have to be elaborate; a simple "thank you" in a meeting, a personal note of appreciation, or highlighting contributions during team discussions can have a profound effect. By consistently valuing input, leaders demonstrate that communication is not transactional but transformational. The importance of adapting communication strategies cannot be overstated. As teams evolve, so do their needs and preferences. What works for a tight-knit group in a small office might not translate for a global team spread across time zones. Leaders must be willing to explore and experiment with new methods, whether it's integrating cutting-edge digital platforms, adjusting meeting formats, or soliciting feedback on existing practices. This adaptability ensures that communication remains effective and relevant, catering to the dynamic nature of today's workplace. Inclusivity in communication also requires acknowledging and accommodating varying styles and preferences. Some team members might thrive in collaborative group settings, while others feel more comfortable expressing their thoughts in one-on-one conversations or written formats. Leaders who are attuned to these differences and willing to flex their approach create an environment where everyone can contribute authentically. By removing communication barriers, leaders amplify the collective intelligence of the team. Feedback is an essential ingredient for continuous improvement in communication. Leaders who embrace feedback as a gift rather than a critique set an example for the entire team. Actively inviting feedback not only shows humility but also encourages a culture of openness. Regularly scheduled surveys, feedback sessions, or even informal conversations can provide valuable insights into what's working and what isn't. But gathering feedback is only half the battle; acting on it is what transforms input into improvement. As much as communication is about sharing information, it's also about creating moments for connection. In a results-driven environment, it's easy to prioritize tasks over relationships. However, taking the time to build relationships pays dividends in the form of trust, camaraderie, and resilience. These moments don't have to be monumental, they could be as simple as checking in with a colleague, remembering a birthday, or sharing a laugh during a meeting. These small acts of connection make it clear that the workplace is more than just a place of business; it's a community. Barriers to communication often manifest in subtle ways, hesitation to speak in meetings, misinterpretation of emails, or reluctance to provide feedback. Leaders must be vigilant in recognizing these signs and proactive in addressing them. This starts with creating an atmosphere of psychological safety, where team members feel confident that speaking their minds will not lead to negative consequences. Psychological safety is the bedrock upon which a culture of open communication is built, and it requires ongoing cultivation through words, actions, and policies. The role of clarity in communication cannot be underestimated. Clarity is not just about being understood, it's about eliminating uncertainty. Whether it's articulating expectations, providing updates, or delivering feedback, clear communication minimizes misunderstandings and ensures alignment. Leaders who prioritize clarity enable their teams to focus on their work with confidence, knowing exactly what is expected and why it matters. While clarity sets the stage, empathy enriches the dialogue. Empathy allows leaders to truly understand the needs, concerns, and aspirations of their team members. It requires listening not just to respond but to comprehend. Empathetic communication builds stronger connections and creates a sense of belonging within the team. By approaching conversations with an open mind and a genuine desire to understand, leaders pave the way for deeper, more meaningful interactions. Conflict is inevitable in any team, but how it is addressed can either strengthen or weaken communication. Leaders who approach conflict with transparency, fairness, and a solutions-oriented mindset model behavior that the rest of the team can emulate. Addressing issues openly and constructively ensures that conflicts become opportunities for growth rather than sources of division. Effective communication is as much about timing as it is about content. Sharing information promptly and proactively prevents rumors, minimizes confusion, and allows the team to address challenges in real time. Leaders who recognize the importance of timing can anticipate the needs of their team and provide the right information at the right moment. Non-verbal communication is another powerful tool in a leader's arsenal. Body language, tone, and eye contact all convey messages that words cannot. By being mindful of these non-verbal cues, leaders can reinforce their spoken words and convey authenticity. This attentiveness creates a sense of presence that strengthens connections during interactions. Celebrating milestones and achievements is an often-overlooked aspect of communication. Whether it's acknowledging the completion of a challenging project or celebrating a work anniversary, these moments reinforce the value of each team member's contributions. Recognition creates positive memories and associations, making the team more cohesive and motivated. Building a strong foundation for communication involves aligning it with the organization's core values. When communication reflects these values, it reinforces the mission and strengthens the culture. Leaders must consistently articulate these values in their messaging and decision-making, ensuring that they are not just words on a wall but principles that guide the team. Innovation thrives in an environment where communication is open and fearless. When team members feel safe to challenge the status quo or propose bold ideas, the organization becomes more adaptable and forward-thinking. Leaders must actively cultivate this environment by encouraging risk-taking and reframing failures as learning opportunities. Communication is a mirror of leadership. When leaders embody the principles of open, honest, and empathetic communication, they inspire the same behaviors in their teams. This alignment creates a culture where everyone feels seen, heard, and valued, setting the stage for extraordinary outcomes. The journey to fostering open communication is one of constant learning and evolution. It's about recognizing that perfection is not the goal; progress is. Every conversation, every gesture, and every decision is an opportunity to strengthen the bonds of trust and understanding within the team. When communication becomes more than just a means to an end, when it becomes the cornerstone of connection, the potential for what the team can achieve together becomes limitless. Regularly revisiting and refining communication practices ensures that they remain effective and relevant to the team's needs. This might involve soliciting feedback on the communication channels in use, experimenting with new tools or techniques, or simply checking in with team members to ensure they feel their voices are being heard. Building a culture of open and honest communication is a multifaceted process that requires deliberate effort, strong leadership, and a commitment to creating an environment where every team member feels safe to speak their mind. By setting the tone for openness, establishing effective communication channels, encouraging two-way dialogue, promoting active listening, and addressing potential barriers, leaders can create a work environment where transparency and honesty are the norms. This culture of open communication not only enhances team cohesion and productivity but also fosters a deeper sense of trust, respect, and mutual understanding among team members.

TIMOTHY K ELLSWORTH

TOGETHER TRIUMPH
Celebrating Every Win.

Celebrating achievements as a team is not just an opportunity to enjoy a moment of joy; it is a powerful strategy for building a cohesive, motivated, and resilient workforce. The act of coming together to acknowledge and celebrate both collective and individual successes plays a crucial role in fostering a positive work environment, where team members feel valued, appreciated, and connected to each other. These celebrations reinforce a family-like culture, where everyone's contributions are recognized, and the shared joy of success strengthens the bonds that tie the team together. This chapter dives into the importance of celebrating wins, how to define what should be celebrated, and the ways to create meaningful and inclusive celebration rituals that boost morale and encourage a culture of continuous improvement. To begin, it is essential to understand the significance of celebrations in the workplace. Celebrations are more than just opportunities to enjoy a break from work or indulge in festivities; they are powerful moments that bring the team together in shared recognition of achievements. When a team celebrates together, it sends a strong message that every effort, whether large or small, is valued. This recognition, boosts morale, and reinforces the connection between individual efforts and team success and motivates everyone to continue striving for excellence. Celebrations provide a sense of closure on completed projects, marking the transition from effort to accomplishment and allowing team members to take pride in their work before moving on to the next challenge. One of the first steps in building a culture of celebration is defining what is worth celebrating. This may seem straightforward, but it requires careful consideration to ensure that the celebrations are meaningful and impactful. While it is natural to celebrate major milestones, such as the successful completion of a significant project or the achievement of company-wide goals, it is equally important to recognize smaller wins that contribute to the overall success of the team. These smaller wins might include reaching a critical deadline, successfully navigating a challenging task, or even personal milestones such as a team member's work anniversary or a promotion. By identifying and celebrating these smaller achievements, leaders can reinforce the idea that every contribution matters, and that success is built from a series of incremental victories. In addition to defining what to celebrate, it is important to establish consistent and meaningful ways to celebrate these wins. The method of celebration should reflect the culture and values of the team, ensuring that it resonates with all members and strengthens the bonds between them. One effective way to do this is by creating celebration rituals, regular, consistent practices that the team can look forward to whenever a win occurs. These rituals can take many forms, depending on the preferences and dynamics of the team. For example, some teams might enjoy celebrating with a shared meal, such as a team lunch or a potluck, where everyone can relax and enjoy each other's company. Others might prefer more formal recognition, such as presenting awards or giving shout-outs during meetings. Whatever the method, the key is to ensure that the celebration feels authentic and inclusive, reflecting the collective spirit of the team. Creating these rituals not only provides a consistent way to celebrate but also helps to build a sense of tradition and identity within the team. Over time, these rituals become part of the team's culture, something that everyone looks forward to and takes pride in. This sense of tradition reinforces the idea that the team is not just a group of individuals working together, but a close-knit community that celebrates its achievements collectively. The anticipation of these celebrations can serve as a motivating factor, encouraging team members to work towards the next milestone with the knowledge that their efforts will be recognized and celebrated. Inclusivity is a crucial element in any celebration. It is essential that celebrations reflect the contributions of all team members, ensuring that everyone feels recognized and valued. This means going beyond simply celebrating the most visible or high-profile achievements and making an effort to acknowledge the contributions of those who might work behind the scenes or in supporting roles. Leaders should be mindful of the diverse ways in which team members contribute to success and ensure that these contributions are highlighted and celebrated. This inclusivity not only fosters a sense of belonging but also encourages a more collaborative and supportive team environment, where everyone feels that their work is important and appreciated. Involving everyone in celebrations also means being mindful of different personalities and preferences within the team. Not everyone may feel comfortable with public recognition or large group events. Some team members may prefer more private or low-key celebrations, such as a personal thank-you note or a small group acknowledgement. Leaders should take the time to understand the preferences of their team members and tailor celebrations to ensure that they are meaningful and enjoyable for everyone involved. This might involve offering different types of recognition or allowing team members to choose how they would like to be celebrated. By respecting individual preferences, leaders can create a more inclusive and positive celebration culture that truly resonates with all team members. While it is important to celebrate wins, it is equally important to balance celebration with a focus on continuous improvement. Celebrations should not signal the end of progress, but rather a moment to pause and reflect before moving forward to the next challenge. This balance can be achieved by framing celebrations within the context of ongoing growth and development. For example, after celebrating the completion of a project, the team might take some time to discuss what went well and what could be improved in the future. This reflection ensures that the team learns from each experience and continues to build on its successes. Leaders can encourage this mindset by celebrating not just the end results, but also the learning and growth that occurred along the way. By doing so, they reinforce the idea that every success is a stepping stone towards even greater achievements. Encouraging peer recognition is another powerful way to build a culture of celebration. While it is important for leaders to recognize and celebrate achievements, it is equally valuable to foster an environment where team members actively recognize and celebrate each other's contributions. Peer recognition can take many forms, from a simple thank-you note or verbal acknowledgment to more formalized systems such as peer-nominated awards or recognition programs. The key is to create a culture where team members feel empowered to celebrate each other's successes and where recognition is seen as a shared responsibility rather than solely the role of leadership. When peers recognize each other's achievements, it strengthens the bonds between team members and creates a more supportive and collaborative environment. To encourage peer recognition, leaders can implement structures or tools that make it easy for team members to acknowledge each other's contributions. This might include setting up a recognition board where team members can post shout-outs or creating a digital platform where achievements can be shared and celebrated. Regularly highlighting examples of peer recognition during team meetings or in communications can also reinforce the importance of this practice and encourage more team members to participate. By making peer recognition a regular part of the team's culture, leaders can foster a more engaged and motivated workforce where everyone feels appreciated and valued. In addition to formal recognition, informal peer recognition is equally important. This can occur spontaneously, in the moment, and often has a powerful impact. A simple word of encouragement, a thank-you for assistance on a task, or an acknowledgement of effort can go a long way in reinforcing positive behaviours and building a culture of appreciation. Encouraging team members to practice this kind of recognition regularly helps to create an environment where gratitude and acknowledgement are woven into the daily fabric of work life. Another important aspect of celebrating wins together is the recognition of personal milestones alongside professional achievements. Workplaces are made up of individuals who bring their whole selves to work, and acknowledging personal milestones, such as birthdays, anniversaries, or personal achievements, helps to build a more holistic and supportive team environment. Celebrating these moments shows that the organization values its team members as individuals, not just for their work contributions. It also helps to build stronger relationships within the team, as members learn more about each other's lives and share in each other's joys and successes. Leaders can support this by creating opportunities for the team to celebrate personal milestones together. This might involve organizing small celebrations, sending cards or gifts, or simply taking the time to acknowledge and congratulate team members during meetings. By incorporating personal milestone celebrations into the team's culture, leaders reinforce the idea that the team is like a family, where everyone's life experiences are valued and celebrated. It's important to recognize that celebrations, while joyful and uplifting, are also an opportunity to reinforce the values and culture of the team. The way in which a team celebrates can reflect and reinforce the principles that guide the organization. For example, if teamwork and collaboration are core values, celebrations might focus on collective achievements and the contributions of the entire team. If innovation and creativity are highly valued, celebrations might highlight moments of ingenuity or breakthroughs. Celebrating milestones and wins does more than just boost morale; it elevates the emotional investment team members have in their shared goals. When we take the time to reflect on collective successes, the acknowledgment creates a shared memory, an anchor point in the team's narrative of achievement. This collective memory becomes something the team can lean on in challenging times, reminding everyone of their capacity to succeed when they come together with determination and effort. Beyond motivation, it builds emotional equity within the team, fostering deeper trust and commitment among its members. Recognition goes beyond a simple pat on the back; it's an opportunity to engage on a deeper level with the team. Celebrations should not feel obligatory or routine, but authentic and reflective of the values that bind the group together. When thoughtfully executed, recognition shows a team member that their work and dedication are truly seen and valued. It creates a ripple effect, where the recognized individual, uplifted by the acknowledgment, is more likely to support and uplift their peers in turn. This virtuous cycle of recognition strengthens the foundation of any team. Sharing achievements shifts the narrative from "me" to "we." This subtle but transformative reframing deepens the collective sense of responsibility and pride within a team. When we celebrate the efforts of others as part of our own journey, we actively dismantle barriers of competition and replace them with collaboration. Team members begin to view their colleagues' successes not as separate or competitive events but as integral contributions to the greater narrative of the team's achievements. The celebration becomes a tangible representation of collective purpose, solidifying that unity. One of the most critical yet often overlooked components of effective celebration is timing. A timely celebration has a profound impact, as it reinforces the connection between effort and acknowledgment. Waiting too long to celebrate a win, risks dulling its significance, potentially losing the momentum it creates. Spontaneous acknowledgment of progress or effort, while maintaining intentionality, bridges the gap between individual and collective motivation. Timing can also emphasize the broader cycle of momentum in the workplace, where progress, recognition, and reward follow each other organically. As leaders and facilitators, there's great value in showcasing consistency in celebration practices. Team members notice when rituals and recognition moments become a staple, transforming the expectation of acknowledgment into a reassurance that their contribution will never go unnoticed. Consistency doesn't dilute the celebration, it enhances its authenticity by embedding it within the team's culture. Predictable, meaningful acknowledgment cultivates the deep psychological safety that allows team members to perform, innovate, and challenge themselves without fear of failure being their sole result. It's worth exploring how methods of celebration can evolve as team dynamics mature. A new team might initially respond best to celebratory gestures that are highly visible, aimed at building rapport and shared experiences. However, as teams develop closer-knit relationships over time, subtler and more personalized acknowledgments may be equally appreciated. Tailoring the way milestones are celebrated ensures that the practice evolves in lockstep with the natural progression of team relationships and dynamics, maintaining its relevancy and impact. Incorporating storytelling into celebrations adds layers of resonance to each win. Sharing narratives of the challenges faced, the teamwork displayed, and the lessons learned transforms each achievement into an inspirational chapter in the team's journey. Stories contextualize individual contributions within broader goals, making every participant feel that their piece of the puzzle was indispensable. When the time to celebrate arises, team members hear these affirmations not only as a result of their work but as motivation for future endeavors. Encouraging active participation during celebrations reinforces inclusivity and engagement. Celebrations become more impactful when team members aren't just passive recipients but active participants. Open forums for recognition, where colleagues can share their gratitude or reflections, turn recognition into a shared experience. It elevates the practice beyond formality, giving each team member a stake in defining their own team culture. The stories shared and gratitude expressed during such moments often illuminate facets of the workplace dynamic that might otherwise go unnoticed. Celebrations also offer a natural opportunity for mentorship. Recognizing wins offers a prime moment to underscore and reward behaviors that align with broader team values and mission. Sharing how an achievement reflects the team's core principles sets an implicit yet powerful example for less experienced members of the group. Simultaneously, it motivates seasoned team members to act as aspirational figures by modeling excellence. Each celebration serves as an echo chamber reinforcing an aligned vision and behavioral standard within the team. Beyond achievement, personal gestures within celebrations elevate the emotional connectivity within a team. Leaders who intentionally personalize a celebration to reflect individual quirks, preferences, or personalities create a sense of being seen in ways that go beyond professional achievement. It may be as simple as referencing a running joke or offering a thoughtful gift specific to an individual's interest. Such personal touches resonate deeply, reminding team members that they're valued not just for what they produce but for who they are. A well-executed celebration can catalyze broader engagement from beyond the core team. For instance, inviting clients or other collaborators to celebrate specific milestones not only recognizes those who are critical to the project but also broadens appreciation across the organizational ecosystem. These "expanded celebrations" foster goodwill, create positive external visibility for the team, and strengthen external relationships in ways that propel both team identity and momentum forward. Reiterating goals and purpose during celebrations helps tether each victory back to the greater mission, giving each achievement a larger sense of consequence. In focusing too much on short-term wins, teams risk compartmentalizing their sense of progress. Acknowledging long-term vision during these moments connects the dots, helping team members understand their own contributions within an unfolding narrative that spans months or even years of effort, collaboration, and execution. By design, celebration cultures transcend work itself and can be applied to resilience-building during challenging times. Just as victories are celebrated, reframing setbacks as learning moments provides valuable opportunities for recalibration and personal acknowledgment. Leaders who create psychological safety around learning experiences help teammates bounce back after difficulty while motivating future contributions to challenging efforts. In doing so, the organization teaches itself not to avoid tough odds but to celebrate every turn of evolution. There is an invisible yet vital aspect of joy to incorporate, the contagious effect celebrations have on group morale long after their initial acknowledgment. Like planting seeds, the act of recognizing a win doesn't cease in the immediate moment but grows in psychological longevity. Positive team memory inevitably comes forward into the "gray" areas of struggle, proving every difficulty as potentially surmountable and transitory. Ingraining celebrations builds resilience with evidence of prior unity and victories. Celebrating success leaves traces across entire work ecosystems, contributing to their emotional health, efficiency, and future creativity. Such recognition raises the standard for what healthy accountability looks like while compelling members within such inclusive environments to act consistently beyond expectations. Recognizing this aggregate cultural impact compels any professional invested in stewardship to preserve, evolve, and yes, joyfully lead those communal rhythms. By aligning celebrations with the team's values, leaders can reinforce these principles and ensure that they are consistently reflected in the team's actions and behaviours. Celebrating wins together is a powerful tool for building a cohesive, motivated, and resilient team. By defining what to celebrate, creating meaningful and inclusive celebration rituals, involving everyone in the process, balancing celebration with continuous improvement, and encouraging peer recognition, leaders can foster a culture where every success is acknowledged, and every team member feels valued. These celebrations not only boost morale and motivation but also strengthen the bonds between team members, creating a work environment where everyone feels connected and committed to the team's success. Ultimately, it is through these shared moments of joy and recognition that a strong, supportive, and unified team culture is built, one that can weather challenges, seize opportunities, and achieve lasting success together.

THE POWER OF US
Teamwork Unleashed

In the modern workplace, where the pace of change is rapid and the demands are high, fostering a culture of collaboration is more crucial than ever. The days when internal competition was seen as the primary driver of success are fading, replaced by the understanding that teamwork and collective effort yield far greater results. While competition can sometimes spur individuals to push harder and achieve more, it often comes at the cost of team cohesion, morale, and long-term success. This chapter dives into the importance of shifting the focus from internal competition to collaboration, where the success of the team as a whole is prioritized over individual achievements. We will explore the downsides of competition, the benefits of promoting team goals, and the strategies for rewarding collaborative efforts, all while providing practical tools and techniques to foster a collaborative mindset among team members. Competition in the workplace, when left unchecked, can create a divisive environment where team members view each other as obstacles to their own success rather than as partners in a shared journey. This mindset can lead to behaviours that undermine trust and teamwork, such as withholding information, taking credit for others' work, or prioritizing personal gains over the collective good. These behaviours, even if unintentional, can damage team dynamics and erode the very foundation of trust and collaboration that a successful team needs. When competition becomes the driving force, the focus shifts from what is best for the team to what is best for the individual, often leading to short-term victories at the expense of long-term success. One of the most significant downsides of competition is its impact on morale. In a competitive environment, team members may feel constant pressure to outperform their colleagues, leading to stress, burnout, and a sense of isolation. Rather than feeling like part of a supportive and united team, individuals may begin to see their coworkers as rivals, creating a toxic atmosphere that stifles creativity and innovation. The emphasis on individual achievement can result in a lack of cohesion, where the team as a whole fails to function as a unified entity. This fragmentation not only hinders productivity but also weakens the team's ability to respond effectively to challenges and changes in the work environment. To counteract the negative effects of competition, it is essential to shift the focus towards collaboration. Promoting team-oriented goals is a powerful way to encourage collaboration and shared success. When goals are set at the team level, rather than individually, it fosters a sense of collective responsibility and accountability. Team members are encouraged to work together, share ideas, and support each other in achieving the common objectives. This collaborative approach not only enhances the quality of the work produced but also strengthens the bonds between team members, creating a more positive and cohesive work environment. In setting team goals, it is important to ensure that these goals are clear, achievable, and aligned with the broader mission of the organization. Leaders play a crucial role in communicating these goals effectively, ensuring that every team member understands how their contributions fit into the larger picture. Regular check-ins and progress updates can help keep the team focused and motivated, while also providing opportunities to address any challenges or obstacles that may arise. By setting goals that require collaboration, leaders can help to shift the mindset from "me" to "we," reinforcing the idea that success is a collective effort. To further promote collaboration, it is important to adjust recognition and rewards systems to highlight and incentivize collaborative efforts. Traditional reward systems often focus on individual achievements, which can inadvertently reinforce competitive behaviour. By contrast, a system that rewards team success and collaborative efforts can encourage team members to prioritize working together over competing against each other. This might include recognizing teams that achieve their goals, rewarding collaborative projects that produce exceptional results, or even celebrating instances where team members have gone out of their way to support each other. In addition to formal recognition, informal recognition plays a critical role in reinforcing collaborative behaviour. Leaders should make it a habit to acknowledge and praise collaborative efforts in real-time, whether it's during meetings, in team communications, or in casual conversations. This kind of immediate, positive reinforcement helps to create a culture where collaboration is valued and encouraged. It also provides a clear signal to the team that working together is not just a requirement, but a key component of their success. Another important aspect of fostering collaboration is the use of tools and techniques that facilitate teamwork and communication. Collaboration tools, such as shared digital platforms, project management software, and communication apps, can help to streamline the collaborative process, making it easier for team members to work together, share information, and stay connected. For example, tools like Slack or Microsoft Teams allow for real-time communication and file sharing, enabling team members to collaborate more effectively, even when working remotely or across different locations. Team brainstorming sessions are another valuable technique for fostering collaboration. These sessions provide a structured opportunity for team members to come together, share ideas, and solve problems collectively. Brainstorming encourages creativity and innovation by allowing team members to build on each other's ideas, rather than working in isolation. To make these sessions most effective, it's important to create an environment where all participants feel comfortable contributing, without fear of judgment or criticism. Leaders can facilitate this by setting clear guidelines for the sessions, encouraging open dialogue, and ensuring that all voices are heard. Implementing collaboration tools and techniques is only part of the solution; it is equally important to cultivate a collaborative mindset among team members.

This involves shifting the underlying attitudes and beliefs that drive behaviour, helping team members to see each other as partners in success rather than competitors. Building a collaborative mindset begins with leadership. Leaders must model collaborative behaviour in their own actions, demonstrating a willingness to work together, share credit, and support their team members. One effective way to build a collaborative mindset is through team-building activities that emphasize cooperation and shared success. These activities, whether they take the form of workshops, retreats, or informal gatherings, provide an opportunity for team members to get to know each other better, build trust, and develop a stronger sense of camaraderie. When team members feel a personal connection with each other, they are more likely to collaborate effectively and support each other in achieving their goals. Another approach to fostering a collaborative mindset is through ongoing training and development. This could include workshops on communication skills, conflict resolution, and teamwork, as well as opportunities for team members to learn new skills together. By investing in the development of the team, leaders send a clear message that collaboration is a priority. Additionally, providing opportunities for cross-functional collaboration, where team members work together on projects that span different areas of the organization, can help to break down silos and promote a more collaborative culture across the board. It is also important to recognize that building a collaborative mindset takes time and requires ongoing effort. Collaboration begins with creating a space where individuals feel safe to voice ideas, concerns, and feedback without fear of dismissal or judgment. This foundational element of psychological safety is indispensable to fostering trust and openness among team members. A team that operates under a shared understanding that all contributions have value creates an environment where creativity flourishes. This trust-building requires active listening, where leaders and team members not only hear but seek to understand the perspectives of others. Such an atmosphere reduces hesitation in sharing innovative ideas, enabling the collective problem-solving process to thrive. As the leader, modeling transparency and vulnerability can profoundly impact team dynamics. By admitting mistakes, seeking input, or openly sharing uncertainties, you set an example that it's okay to be human. When others see this, they are encouraged to follow suit, lowering barriers that often restrict authentic collaboration. This openness must be coupled with an unwavering commitment to finding solutions together, highlighting that every individual is accountable for the collective success or failure of the team. It creates a culture where failure is viewed as an opportunity for growth rather than a trigger for blame. A central tenet of fostering collaboration is identifying and leveraging the unique strengths and skills of each team member. Often, leaders focus on ensuring equality in workload distribution without fully tapping into the individuality of their teams. A nuanced approach involves aligning tasks and responsibilities with each person's strengths, ensuring that their contributions shine. Doing so not only enhances productivity but also helps team members feel appreciated for what makes them uniquely valuable.

When individuals are acknowledged for their expertise and allowed to take ownership of certain aspects of a project, the resulting synergy propels the team forward. Leaders must also address and dismantle hidden barriers to collaboration, which often stem from long-standing workplace silos or personal biases. Silos, whether departmental or cultural, can stagnate information flow and impede innovation. It requires deliberate efforts to break down these walls, ensuring that information and resources are accessible to all. Facilitating interdepartmental projects or encouraging diverse team compositions can challenge preconceived notions, bringing together a variety of perspectives. This intentional mixing fosters empathy, understanding, and respect among team members, key ingredients for collaboration to flourish. While creating collaboration opportunities, it is important to balance structure with flexibility. Teams thrive when given clear objectives, defined roles, and timelines, but they also need autonomy to approach tasks creatively. Micromanagement suffocates the collaborative spirit, as it signals a lack of trust in the team's capabilities. Conversely, excessive freedom without direction can lead to chaos. Finding the equilibrium allows teams to move cohesively toward common goals while innovating within the parameters of their responsibilities. This balance enables teams to stay accountable to each other and their objectives without unnecessary constraints. Purpose plays a pivotal role in inspiring teams to collaborate at a deeper level. When every member of a team understands how their work contributes to the larger mission or vision of an organization, it provides motivation beyond mere task completion. Leaders must articulate this purpose clearly and frequently, weaving it into the daily narrative of the team's work. Aligning individual responsibilities with the broader impact encourages a sense of belonging, reminding team members that their efforts serve something greater than themselves. Purpose-driven collaboration has the power to transform the mundane into the meaningful. One challenge in collaboration is ensuring that every voice is heard, particularly in diverse teams where differences in communication styles or cultural backgrounds might cause some perspectives to be overlooked. It's the responsibility of the leader to proactively create opportunities for quieter members to contribute without putting undue pressure on them. Structured discussions, anonymous suggestion channels, and smaller breakout groups can help ensure everyone's input is valued. Celebrating the contributions of all members, not just the most vocal, demonstrates an appreciation for diverse thinking and encourages broader engagement. Conflict is an inevitable aspect of collaboration and, when managed correctly, can serve as a catalyst for growth and innovation. Healthy disagreement fosters a more robust exchange of ideas, enabling the team to arrive at better solutions than a single individual could achieve alone. As a leader, facilitating constructive conflict involves mediating when necessary and teaching the team to debate respectfully. Clear communication, combined with mutual respect and trust, ensures that disagreements do not devolve into personal conflicts. Instead, they become opportunities to refine ideas and strengthen team cohesion. Recognizing incremental progress is a powerful motivator in sustaining collaboration. It's easy to focus solely on the end goal, but small wins along the way validate the team's efforts and reinforce the idea that collaboration yields results. Leaders should be deliberate in celebrating these milestones, framing them within the context of the collective contributions that made them possible. Whether it's an email shoutout, a quick team huddle, or even a more formal recognition, these moments of acknowledgment can energize the team for the next phase of their journey. Leaders must remain attuned to the shifting dynamics within their teams. Collaboration is not a static process; it requires ongoing adjustments based on factors such as team growth, turnover, or evolving objectives. Regularly taking the pulse of the team through surveys, one-on-one conversations, or group reflections helps leaders identify areas where adjustments are needed. Creating a feedback loop ensures the team feels heard and can pivot together as challenges arise. These responsive adjustments not only maintain the collaborative spirit but also reinforce a culture of adaptability and resilience. Investing in personal and professional growth opportunities for team members creates a fertile ground for collaboration. People who feel stagnant in their roles are less likely to engage fully in team efforts. Training sessions, mentorship opportunities, and access to skill-building resources benefit both individuals and the collective group. When team members grow individually, their contributions to the team also grow, creating a virtuous cycle of shared progress. Furthermore, enabling cross-functional training fosters understanding and appreciation of other roles, reducing barriers to collaboration. The physical or virtual environment in which a team operates can significantly impact their ability to collaborate effectively. Spaces designed to encourage interaction, whether it's through open layouts or digital platforms that facilitate seamless communication, reinforce a team's ability to work together. Equally important is ensuring that these spaces support focused work when needed. Hybrid work environments offer a unique challenge, requiring tools and practices that connect remote and in-office team members equally. Thoughtful design and resource allocation play a critical role in enabling collaboration in any setting. Embracing vulnerability and imperfection as a leader lays the groundwork for teams to embrace their own. When individuals feel they have the freedom to fail without severe repercussions, they are more willing to take risks that could lead to breakthroughs. A collaborative environment flourishes when risk-taking is encouraged and supported by the team. Leaders must set an example by framing failures as learning opportunities, reinforcing the notion that the process is as important as the outcome. This mindset fosters a shared resilience that strengthens bonds among team members. Storytelling is an often-underutilized tool in fostering collaboration. Sharing stories of past successes achieved through teamwork serves as both inspiration and a roadmap for future efforts. These narratives highlight the value of each role within the team, underscoring that no one individual achieves greatness alone. Stories can also humanize leadership and cultivate deeper connections among team members, making collaboration feel less transactional and more relational. By integrating storytelling into team meetings, workshops, or even casual conversations, leaders instill a shared identity rooted in the power of collective effort. The legacy of collaboration lies not just in the projects completed or goals achieved it lies in the relationships and skills developed along the way. A team that has learned to collaborate effectively carries those abilities into every future endeavor, creating a ripple effect throughout the organization. These teams are equipped to tackle unforeseen challenges, innovate beyond expectations, and support one another through adversity. As a leader, the most rewarding aspect of fostering collaboration is witnessing the transformation of a group of individuals into a unified, high-performing team that continues to thrive long after their initial objectives are met. Leaders must be patient and persistent in their efforts to shift the team's focus from competition to collaboration. This might involve addressing and overcoming resistance to change, particularly from team members who are accustomed to a more competitive environment. Open communication is key in this process. Leaders should engage in regular dialogue with their team, discussing the benefits of collaboration, addressing any concerns or challenges, and reinforcing the importance of working together towards common goals. Shifting the focus from internal competition to collaboration is essential for building a unified, high-performing team. While competition can drive short-term results, it often comes at the expense of long-term success, undermining trust, morale, and team cohesion. By promoting team goals, rewarding collaborative efforts, implementing effective tools and techniques, and cultivating a collaborative mindset, leaders can create a work environment where team members see each other as partners in success, rather than competitors. This shift not only enhances the team's ability to achieve its goals but also fosters a more positive, supportive, and cohesive work culture. Collaboration stands as the cornerstone of a thriving team, where individuals combine their unique strengths and perspectives to address challenges with creativity and resilience. By working together, teams can navigate complexities more effectively, uncover hidden opportunities, and drive innovation in ways that solitary effort cannot achieve. The spirit of collaboration fosters an environment where mutual support and shared vision inspire team members to reach beyond personal limitations, achieving goals that feel both ambitious and attainable. This unified approach not only propels organizations toward long-term success but also cultivates a positive culture where trust, respect, and collective effort become the foundations for sustained growth and excellence. Through the power of collaboration, teams can break down barriers, unlock their full potential, and achieve outcomes that resonate far beyond the sum of their individual contributions.

TIMOTHY K ELLSWORTH

WHERE TRUST LEADS
Teams Succeed

In the intricate web of relationships that define a successful workplace, trust stands as the cornerstone. It is the invisible yet powerful force that binds a team together, fostering a sense of security, openness, and mutual respect. Without trust, even the most skilled teams can falter, as mistrust breeds miscommunication, inefficiency, and discord. In contrast, when trust is deeply ingrained in a team's culture, it paves the way for collaboration, innovation, and resilience. This chapter dives into the vital importance of trust in the workplace, exploring how leaders can establish, nurture, and, when necessary, rebuild trust within their teams. By understanding and prioritizing trust, organizations can create a family-like work culture where every member feels valued, supported, and empowered to contribute their best. Trust is not a superficial element of team dynamics; it is foundational. It forms the bedrock upon which all other aspects of teamwork are built, influencing everything from communication and collaboration to morale and productivity. Trust enables team members to rely on one another, to feel confident that their contributions are valued, and to believe that their colleagues have their best interests at heart. When trust is present, it creates a sense of safety, allowing team members to take risks, share ideas, and engage in honest, constructive dialogue without fear of judgment or retaliation. This environment of trust is essential for fostering a positive work culture, where team members feel genuinely connected to each other and to the organization's mission. The importance of trust in a team cannot be overstated. It is the glue that holds the team together, enabling effective communication, collaboration, and problem-solving. When trust is strong, team members are more likely to share information freely, seek input from others, and work together towards common goals. This openness and willingness to collaborate lead to better decision-making, as diverse perspectives are considered and integrated into the final outcome. Trust also enhances morale, as team members feel supported and respected, which in turn leads to higher levels of engagement and job satisfaction. In contrast, a lack of trust can create a toxic work environment, where team members are guarded, reluctant to share information, and more concerned with protecting themselves than with contributing to the team's success. For leaders, building trust begins with leading by example. Trust is not something that can be mandated; it must be earned through consistent, ethical behavior and transparent decision-making. Leaders who demonstrate integrity in their actions, who communicate openly and honestly, and who follow through on their commitments set the tone for the rest of the team. When leaders model these behaviours, they create a culture where trust can flourish.

This means being transparent about decision-making processes, explaining the reasons behind certain choices, and being honest about challenges and uncertainties. By being open and forthcoming, leaders show that they respect their team members enough to include them in the conversation, which in turn fosters trust. Integrity is a key component of trust-building. Leaders who act with integrity are consistent in their words and actions, upholding ethical standards even when it is difficult or unpopular to do so. This consistency builds credibility, as team members know they can rely on their leaders to act fairly and responsibly. Integrity also involves accountability, leaders must be willing to take responsibility for their actions, admit when they are wrong, and make amends when necessary. This willingness to own up to mistakes and learn from them demonstrates humility and builds trust, as team members see that their leaders are not only human but also committed to doing what is right. Another crucial element of trust-building is encouraging open and honest communication. Communication is the lifeblood of any team, and when it is rooted in honesty and openness, it strengthens the bonds of trust. Leaders can promote this by creating an environment where team members feel safe to speak their minds, share their ideas, and express their concerns. This means actively listening to team members, valuing their input, and responding with empathy and understanding. It also means being transparent in communications, sharing information openly, and avoiding the temptation to withhold or manipulate information for personal or organizational gain. When communication is open and honest, it builds trust by ensuring that everyone is on the same page, working towards the same goals, and aware of the challenges and opportunities that lie ahead. Trust is not just built through words; it is also built through actions. One of the most effective ways to build trust within a team is through team-building activities and exercises. These activities provide an opportunity for team members to connect on a personal level, to learn more about each other's strengths and weaknesses, and to build the kind of relationships that form the foundation of trust. Team-building activities can take many forms, from structured exercises that focus on communication and collaboration to more informal social events that allow team members to bond outside of the work environment. The key is to create opportunities for team members to interact in ways that build mutual respect, understanding, and trust. For example, activities that require team members to work together to solve a problem or complete a task can help to build trust by highlighting the importance of collaboration and the value of each team member's contributions. These activities also provide an opportunity for team members to see each other in a different light, to recognize and appreciate the unique skills and perspectives that each person brings to the table. Over time, these shared experiences build a sense of camaraderie and trust that carries over into the team's day-to-day work, making it easier to collaborate, communicate, and achieve shared goals. However, building trust is not a one-time effort; it requires ongoing attention and effort. Trust must be maintained over time, and leaders must be vigilant in ensuring that it is not eroded by misunderstandings, miscommunications, or unethical behaviour. This means regularly reinforcing the importance of trust, both through words and actions, and addressing any issues that arise promptly and effectively. Leaders should be proactive in seeking feedback from their team members, asking how they can better support them and build trust within the team. By being open to feedback and willing to make changes, leaders demonstrate their commitment to maintaining trust and creating a positive work environment. Despite the best efforts, there may be times when trust is broken, either due to a mistake, a miscommunication, or a breach of integrity. When this happens, it is crucial to address the issue head-on and take steps to rebuild trust. Rebuilding trust is not easy, and it requires a sincere commitment to making things right. This begins with acknowledging the breach of trust, taking responsibility for the actions that led to it, and apologizing to those who were affected. It is important that this apology is genuine and accompanied by a clear plan for how the issue will be addressed and prevented in the future. Once the initial steps have been taken to address the breach of trust, it is important to focus on rebuilding the relationship. This may involve having open and honest conversations with the individuals involved, addressing any lingering concerns, and finding ways to restore confidence in the relationship. It may also involve making changes to processes or behaviours to ensure that the same issue does not arise again. Trust is often invisible but undeniably felt, like the foundation of a structure that determines its strength and longevity. In the context of a team, trust is not just a concept but a practice, a dynamic, ever-evolving quality that must be cultivated and nurtured over time. It begins in the simple things: delivering on promises, showing respect for others' opinions, and displaying genuine care for the well-being of the team. These seemingly small acts create a ripple effect, deepening connections among team members. When individuals know they can rely on one another, barriers break down, paving the way for transparency, openness, and collaboration. Trust doesn't happen by accident; it is built brick by brick, interaction by interaction, as leaders and team members engage with honesty and integrity. The role of trust becomes particularly evident when teams face adversity. During challenging times, trust serves as a stabilizing force that keeps everyone aligned and focused on shared goals. In moments of uncertainty, individuals who trust their teammates are more likely to rally together, offering support and innovative solutions. The absence of trust, however, can magnify issues, with miscommunication and mistrust breeding frustration and conflict. Leaders who prioritize trust build a reservoir of goodwill that teams can draw upon in times of need. This reservoir is not unlimited but replenished through consistent actions that reflect fairness, empathy, and respect. In fostering a high-trust environment, leaders can transform potential crises into opportunities for unity and growth. Communication is where trust is most visibly tested and demonstrated. Open, transparent, and two-way communication is both a signal and a byproduct of a trusting relationship. Within a team, it's the act of speaking honestly and listening intently that strengthens trust, making individuals feel heard, valued, and respected. Leaders must foster a culture where expressing concerns or admitting mistakes is seen as a strength, not a weakness. This begins with listening, not just hearing, but truly understanding the perspectives of others. When team members feel understood, they are more willing to open up, which deepens interpersonal trust. Leaders can take it further by providing regular updates, sharing the rationale behind decisions, and ensuring that everyone is informed, eliminating the seeds of doubt and speculation that could compromise trust. Trust thrives in a culture of inclusivity and appreciation. When team members feel valued for their unique contributions, trust naturally deepens. This doesn't mean treating everyone the same; it means recognizing and celebrating the distinct strengths and talents each person brings to the table. As individuals contribute in their own ways, they also build confidence in one another, realizing that every member plays an essential role in achieving shared objectives. Demonstrating appreciation, whether through a simple thank-you or a public acknowledgment of effort, goes a long way in affirming mutual respect and value. An inclusive and appreciative environment not only fosters trust but also inspires team members to invest their energy and creativity wholeheartedly, knowing their contributions truly matter. Decision-making offers another arena where trust either flourishes or falters. Leaders who involve their teams in decisions, where appropriate, send a strong message: "I trust your judgment, and your perspective matters." This inclusivity empowers team members to take ownership of outcomes, knowing that their voices shape the direction of the group. Trust also means being transparent about the decision-making process, explaining how choices align with team or organizational values. On the other hand, withholding information or making decisions in isolation erodes trust, leaving team members feeling undervalued and excluded. When leaders consistently demonstrate that decisions are made ethically, thoughtfully, and with the team's best interests at heart, trust becomes a natural byproduct of those choices. Accountability is one of the clearest demonstrations of trust in action. In a trusting team, accountability is not about assigning blame but taking collective and individual responsibility for successes and setbacks alike. Leaders set the tone by being transparent about their own missteps and modeling how to accept responsibility with humility. When a team sees its leader take ownership of errors, they are more likely to embrace accountability themselves. This reinforces trust within the group, as members know they can count on each other to own their actions and learn from mistakes. In an accountable environment, trust creates a safety net where experimentation and honest dialogue can thrive, transforming failures into valuable lessons. Boundaries also play an important role in building and maintaining trust. Establishing clear expectations regarding roles, responsibilities, and goals provides a framework that allows individuals to focus on collaboration without the confusion of overlapping or unclear tasks. When these boundaries are set, they signal respect for the capabilities and autonomy of each team member. Leaders who are mindful of these boundaries encourage confidence among team members, as everyone understands their own contributions and trusts others to fulfill their commitments. This clarity not only reduces potential conflicts but also creates an atmosphere where trust can grow organically, rooted in mutual understanding and respect. Conflict, though often seen as negative, presents unique opportunities to strengthen trust when addressed constructively. Healthy conflict, rooted in respect and a shared commitment to success, fosters open dialogue and collaborative problem-solving. Leaders play a crucial role in guiding these moments of tension, ensuring they remain productive and focused. Addressing conflict with empathy, impartiality, and a focus on solutions demonstrates fairness and builds trust within the team. It reassures individuals that their voices matter and that differences of opinion are valued. Over time, navigating conflict effectively reinforces trust by proving that the team can overcome disagreements without compromising relationships or collective goals. Leadership in a trust-based culture involves active mentorship and support. By consistently investing in the personal and professional growth of team members, leaders build a legacy of trust that extends beyond immediate tasks. Whether through providing opportunities for skill development, offering constructive feedback, or advocating for their team's needs, leaders create an environment where individuals feel genuinely cared for. This support not only builds trust in the leader's intentions but also strengthens the bonds between team members, as they see their leader prioritize collective well-being over personal gain. A culture of support and mentorship transforms trust into an enduring organizational asset. Celebrating shared successes fosters trust by reminding teams of their collective strength. Recognizing achievements, whether large or small, reinforces the idea that collaboration and mutual trust lead to tangible, meaningful results. Leaders should make it a point to highlight how trust and cooperation contributed to successes, encouraging teams to continue cultivating those qualities. Public celebrations and private acknowledgments alike demonstrate that every effort matters, and every individual is seen, further solidifying the trust that binds the group. Trust in the workplace goes beyond individual relationships and can become a guiding principle for the entire organization. When trust is engrained in the organizational culture, it creates a framework for decision-making, communication, and problem-solving that extends throughout all levels of the company. Leaders can encourage this by ensuring that trust-building efforts are embedded in everything, from strategic planning to day-to-day interactions. By making trust an explicit organizational value, leaders signal to team members that it is not only accepted but expected. When every member, from the newest hire to the CEO, is encouraged to contribute and trusted to perform, the organization operates at its fullest potential. Trust helps break down silos, fosters cross-departmental collaboration, and amplifies the collective strength of the organization. The transparency that supports trust needs to be not only consistent but context sensitive. Leaders must recognize that each team and individual will have different needs for information and involvement, and tailoring communication to match these needs is essential. Being transparent doesn't mean oversharing or divulging every detail; it means sharing enough so that team members feel informed, aligned, and trusted to act. By regularly checking in with team members to gauge their understanding and needs, leaders can refine their approach to communication, ensuring that trust is built on a foundation of relevance and clarity. In cases where ambiguity is unavoidable, leaders who demonstrate the ability to communicate with honesty and vulnerability allow their teams to see their decision-making process at work, which strengthens trust further. Rebuilding trust after it is damaged can feel like an insurmountable challenge, but it is not impossible. The key to rebuilding trust is acknowledging the pain, both personal and collective, that a breach creates. This involves creating space for open conversations, giving individuals an opportunity to express their feelings and concerns without fear of judgment or retaliation. Leaders must show that they are actively invested in repairing the relationship by apologizing sincerely and making visible changes that demonstrate their commitment to regaining trust. These changes might involve revisiting team dynamics, implementing new processes for transparency, or simply making a greater effort to be present and involved with team members. Rebuilding takes time, and leaders must remain consistent and patient, steadily rebuilding trust one action at a time, until the team sees that the relationship has been restored and strengthened. Beyond transparency and vulnerability, another vital component in nurturing trust is consistency. Trust thrives in an environment where expectations are clear, and behaviors align with those expectations over time. A leader's ability to deliver consistent messaging and decisions ensures that team members can predict how they will respond in various situations, giving them a sense of stability and confidence. This consistency helps remove uncertainties that could otherwise breed distrust. A leader who is unpredictable or who flips between opposing decisions will quickly lose the confidence of their team. Trust, on the other hand, grows steadily as leaders exhibit reliability in their decisions, showing their teams that they can be counted on to act with integrity, fairness, and dependability over the long haul. Trust in the workplace goes hand in hand with emotional intelligence. Leaders with high emotional intelligence understand the emotional dynamics of their teams, enabling them to respond effectively to individuals' feelings and concerns. Empathy, self-awareness, and emotional regulation help foster deeper relationships between team members and their leaders. By being attuned to the emotions in the room, leaders can navigate delicate situations with the care and understanding needed to sustain trust. Emotional intelligence creates a safe environment for people to express their thoughts and emotions, confident that they will be heard and respected. When leaders can connect with their team members on an emotional level, it's easier to navigate conflict, make informed decisions, and sustain trust even in difficult times. Rebuilding trust takes time, and it requires patience, persistence, and a willingness to be vulnerable. Maintaining trust over the long term requires a commitment to ongoing communication, integrity, and accountability. Leaders must continue to model the behaviours that build trust, such as transparency, honesty, and ethical decision-making. They must also be vigilant in addressing any issues that arise, ensuring that trust is not eroded by misunderstandings, conflicts, or unethical behaviour. By making trust a central focus of their leadership, and by fostering a culture of openness and accountability, leaders can create a work environment where trust is strong, and where team members feel valued, supported, and empowered to do their best work. Building trust across the team is essential for creating a cohesive, positive, and high-performing work environment. Trust is the foundation upon which all other aspects of teamwork are built, and without it, even the most talented teams can struggle to achieve their potential. By leading with integrity, encouraging open and honest communication, using team-building activities to strengthen relationships, and maintaining trust over time, leaders can create a culture of trust that supports collaboration, innovation, and success. Trust is not something that can be taken for granted; it must be nurtured, protected, and, when necessary, rebuilt. By prioritizing trust, leaders can create an environment where team members feel engaged and empowered to contribute their best.

TIMOTHY K ELLSWORTH

THE PRAISE EFFECT
Powering Up Recognition

In the intricate dance of team dynamics, recognition and appreciation play a critical role in maintaining morale, boosting motivation, and fostering a strong sense of belonging. When team members feel genuinely valued for their contributions, they are more likely to be engaged, productive, and committed to the organization's success. A culture of recognition goes beyond occasional praise; it is about embedding appreciation into the daily fabric of work life so that every team member feels seen, heard, and valued. This chapter explores the essential components of building a culture of recognition, including how to make recognition personal and meaningful, the importance of peer-to-peer appreciation, recognizing effort as well as outcomes, and ensuring that recognition is both visible and inclusive. Creating a culture of recognition begins with the understanding that recognition is not a luxury or an afterthought; it is a fundamental part of building a positive and productive work environment. In a culture where recognition is valued, team members understand that their contributions, no matter how big or small, will be noticed and appreciated. This kind of environment fosters a sense of ownership and pride in one's work, as well as a deeper connection to the team and its goals. It also helps to reduce turnover, as employees who feel valued are less likely to seek validation and appreciation elsewhere. To develop such a culture, recognition must be made a regular, expected part of work life. This means moving beyond sporadic or ad hoc acknowledgments and creating systems and routines that ensure recognition happens consistently. For example, some organizations implement weekly or monthly recognition rituals, where team members gather to celebrate achievements, milestones, and contributions. These rituals can take many forms, from formal award ceremonies to more informal gatherings where team members share praise and gratitude. The key is to establish a rhythm of recognition that is consistent and reliable, so that team members come to expect and look forward to these moments of appreciation. However, creating a culture of recognition is not just about frequency; it is also about quality. Recognition should not be generic or impersonal; it should be tailored to the individual, reflecting their unique contributions and preferences. Personalizing recognition means taking the time to understand what each team member values and how they like to be acknowledged. For some, public recognition might be motivating and affirming, while others might prefer a private note or one-on-one conversation. By tailoring recognition to individual preferences, leaders can ensure that their appreciation is meaningful and impactful, rather than just another checkbox on a list. Personalizing recognition also involves acknowledging the specific contributions that an individual has made, rather than offering vague or general praise. Instead of simply saying, "Good job," leaders should strive to highlight what exactly was done well and why it was important. For example, instead of saying, "Thanks for your hard work," a more personalized approach might be, "Thank you for staying late to ensure that the project was completed on time. Your dedication and attention to detail made all the difference." This kind of specific recognition not only makes the individual feel valued but also reinforces the behaviors and actions that the organization wants to encourage. While recognition from leaders is important, peer-to-peer recognition can be equally, if not more, powerful. When team members take the initiative to recognize and appreciate each other, it fosters a sense of camaraderie and mutual respect. It also helps to create an environment where recognition is seen as a collective responsibility, rather than something that is solely the domain of management. Encouraging peer-to-peer recognition can be as simple as setting up systems that make it easy for team members to acknowledge each other's contributions. This could include tools like recognition boards, where team members can post notes of appreciation, or digital platforms where colleagues can send shout-outs or kudos. To promote peer-to-peer recognition, leaders can model the behavior by regularly recognizing their peers and encouraging others to do the same. They can also create opportunities for peer recognition to take place, such as dedicating a portion of team meetings to sharing appreciation or setting up regular peer-nominated awards. By making peer recognition a visible and valued part of the team culture, leaders can help to build a more supportive and collaborative work environment, where everyone feels appreciated and valued by their colleagues. It is also important to recognize that appreciation should not be reserved only for successful outcomes. While celebrating achievements is important, it is equally crucial to recognize the effort, hard work, and persistence that team members put into their tasks, even when the outcome is not as expected. By acknowledging the effort, leaders send a powerful message that they value dedication and perseverance, and that the journey is just as important as the destination. This approach not only motivates team members to continue striving for success but also helps to create a more resilient and adaptable team, where failure is seen as an opportunity for growth rather than a source of shame. Recognizing effort also involves understanding and appreciating the different ways that team members contribute to the success of the team. Not all contributions are visible or easily measurable, but that does not make them any less valuable. For example, someone who consistently fosters a positive and supportive work environment, or who quietly mentors and supports their colleagues, might not always receive the recognition they deserve. Leaders should make an effort to identify and acknowledge these less visible contributions, ensuring that all forms of effort and dedication are recognized and appreciated. Making recognition visible and inclusive is another key aspect of building a culture of appreciation. Recognition should be something that is celebrated openly, so that all team members can share in the joy and feel inspired by each other's successes. This does not mean that every recognition needs to be a grand public event, but rather that there should be opportunities for team members to be acknowledged in a way that is visible to their peers. This could include public shout-outs during meetings, recognition newsletters, or even a dedicated section in the company's digital communication platform. Inclusivity in recognition means ensuring that everyone, regardless of their role, background, or personality, has the opportunity to be recognized and celebrated. Recognition should not simply be an afterthought in our work culture, but an intentional part of daily life. It means continually finding ways to acknowledge our team members in such a way that it resonates with them as individuals. Tailored recognition brings deeper connection and appreciation, where each gesture feels genuine and authentic. The act of acknowledging effort, no matter how big or small, contributes not only to that specific team member's sense of purpose but to the morale of the entire group. Consistent recognition drives long-term motivation and fosters loyalty within the team. Whether it's publicly acknowledging someone's hard work or sending a private thank-you note, the key is making the recognition purposeful, connecting it to something meaningful the person has done, and making the effort known in such a way that it resonates with the recipient. By embedding recognition into every interaction and meeting, it becomes part of the fabric of the team's culture. It's about establishing a rhythm of acknowledgment, where recognition becomes an expected and celebrated routine, much like a vital thread in a well-woven tapestry. An environment where regular recognition is the norm not only ensures that no one feels unnoticed but also allows individuals to actively participate in the recognition process. When we embrace a continuous rhythm, from the smallest acknowledgment to major celebrations, we create a tone where appreciation is deeply embedded in every aspect of the team's life. This rhythm also forms a model that team members can follow themselves, perpetuating a cycle of praise and gratitude that ripples throughout the workplace, creating an environment built on respect, trust, and shared success. A crucial element of fostering a truly effective culture of recognition is ensuring that it becomes a visible and recognized value, not only celebrated within team spaces but extended across the organization. Visibility encourages everyone to witness the impact and reinforces the fact that contributions, even behind the scenes, are equally valued. Highlighting the recognition of individuals encourages others to think about their unique contributions and how they can show respect to their colleagues as well. It elevates the collective spirit of the team and ensures that no one goes unnoticed for the essential work they do. Making recognition visible goes beyond mere praise, it's about creating tangible, shared moments where appreciation becomes an interactive, collective activity that engages not only the recipients but also those who witness it. One overlooked yet significant aspect of recognition lies in its ability to promote inclusivity across the team. When leaders create opportunities where recognition transcends personal preferences and involves every member of the organization, it ensures no one feels like an outsider. Recognition, when done with genuine inclusivity in mind, provides those who may not often take center stage with the same regard for their contributions as their more vocal counterparts. By recognizing the various ways in which people contribute, whether through quiet support or visible leadership, a sense of balance and fairness arises within the team. Creating an inclusive environment means acknowledging the diverse ways people express value and fostering an atmosphere in which every contribution feels heard, seen, and celebrated. Giving credit where it's due is just as important as the acknowledgment itself. We must ensure that we not only recognize individual successes but the impact of collaboration. By nurturing an environment where shared success is celebrated, we elevate team unity and remove the barriers that hinder effective teamwork. Recognition is a powerful tool that should encourage continued collaboration. It's a tool for inspiring each person to think less of the individual spotlight and more about what we as a team can achieve. Whether it's the engineer who troubleshoots issues after hours or the administrator who manages schedules, the recognition that people receive shouldn't solely focus on the final product but highlight the commitment, sacrifices, and teamwork behind each step forward. Reflecting on the contributions made by those working behind the scenes is vital to ensuring that every part of the machine is acknowledged. Often, the individuals who are pivotal in day-to-day operations do not receive the recognition they deserve for the consistent maintenance of momentum. They can be the quiet but steady sources of support, the ones who keep things running smoothly even when the focus is elsewhere. Acknowledging their contributions reinforces the idea that no one's work, no matter its visibility, goes unnoticed. This recognition makes it clear that even the smallest contributions matter, and that everyone plays a role in bringing the bigger picture to life. By ensuring everyone has the space and encouragement to voice what they've achieved, we empower them to continue their integral contributions and foster deeper team unity. Effort, as much as outcome, must be a focal point in fostering a recognition culture. There are moments when the outcome isn't perfect but where an immense effort has been poured in. Recognizing the hustle, the sleepless nights, and the passion that drive progress is essential to building a supportive and resilient team culture. When leaders spotlight effort in tandem with result, they underscore that success isn't defined only by perfection or completion but by the relentless pursuit of progress. This method helps discourage the fear of failure and invites a mindset shift, one that views every setback not as a personal flaw but as a stepping stone in growth. Recognizing effort also gives rise to an adaptive, fearless team, where failure is seen not as a disappointment but as a valuable learning process. Celebrating both success and effort encourages a growth mindset across the organization. By placing equal value on what is learned in the pursuit of a goal as on the end result itself, the team learns to embrace challenges and develop resilience. Teams will feel encouraged to attempt more ambitious projects when they know that effort and intent will also be acknowledged. Creating an environment where effort is rewarded helps to build emotional resilience, foster continuous growth, and fuel intrinsic motivation. Leaders can guide this mindset by balancing their praise for finished projects with deep respect for the persistent work and learning that lead up to that success, signaling that they are equally invested in the journey of growth and exploration. With an increasingly diverse workforce, it's more important than ever to recognize the varied ways in which individuals contribute. Not everyone works the same way, and recognizing these differences ensures that everyone feels understood and valued for their unique contributions. Diverse personalities and work styles require a customized approach to recognition, one where the specifics of what drives each individual's motivation are considered. Through inclusive recognition, we also send the message that it's okay to be different and that diversity doesn't detract from value, it enriches it. Tailoring recognition allows every team member to feel like they belong in a space where they are uniquely seen for who they are and what they bring to the table, enhancing the team's overall cohesiveness and effectiveness. Flexibility in how recognition is delivered makes it more meaningful and authentic. For some, a brief and thoughtful message is all they need to feel truly appreciated, while others might thrive on public acknowledgment in front of their peers. By giving space for this flexibility, recognition evolves into a tool that strengthens personal bonds rather than creating a rigid system. Each person's relationship to recognition is distinct, so finding ways to understand and reflect this is one of the hallmarks of great leadership. Leaders should be mindful of these preferences, engaging in regular dialogue to determine the methods and means that best align with each individual. This attention to personalized recognition promotes an environment where each person's unique value is magnified, contributing to greater engagement and satisfaction. There is also great power in vulnerability within recognition. By acknowledging that we too experience challenges and limitations, we help build a foundation of mutual respect and understanding. Openly recognizing the collective effort, regardless of how complex or demanding the work was, helps the team feel more at ease with their own vulnerabilities. In sharing our challenges, leaders reinforce that the act of acknowledgment isn't about perfection, but about growing together. When leaders reveal the ways in which they also rely on the team, it fosters an environment where collective success is truly about supporting one another through all situations, triumphs and setbacks alike. As recognition becomes a shared journey, we begin to establish greater empathy and connection across the team, allowing trust to flourish within the organization. Having a solid structure for recognition gives it continuity and stability, making it an ongoing pillar within team dynamics. The importance of not letting recognition fall to the wayside, particularly during busy or challenging periods, cannot be overstated. Creating a set of recognizable, predictable moments for acknowledgment, whether through periodic meetings, recognition programs, or simple team check-ins, allows the practice of recognizing efforts to become non-negotiable. As teams grow and change, revisiting the methods of appreciation can bring consistency and help connect individual contributions to the larger picture, ensuring that those who are putting in the effort, however silently, feel woven into the fabric of the team's culture and objectives. Having systems in place for sustainable recognition helps maintain momentum even when organizational focus shifts, keeping appreciation consistent no matter the operational environment. Leaders must also continuously reassess their recognition strategies to ensure they resonate with the ever-evolving team dynamic. What worked well in one phase of growth or with one team member might need tweaking as new projects arise and the team culture changes. Staying attuned to the needs, goals, and values of individual team members and the group as a whole ensures that recognition remains relevant and engaging. This constant adjustment helps the team stay motivated by evolving their understanding of recognition and appreciating that leadership is taking steps to keep appreciation fresh and meaningful. When recognition feels relevant, it fosters a deeper sense of pride in one's work, ensuring that teams stay focused on both the organization's long-term mission and their personal growth along the journey. Including team members in the decision-making process when it comes to recognition strategies promotes buy-in and a stronger commitment to the culture. When employees have input into the ways in which recognition is delivered, they feel a sense of ownership over the process, which heightens the impact of the recognition. This inclusion encourages transparency within the team, where members are aware of why recognition occurs the way it does and can offer insights into what makes it more meaningful. By empowering the team to shape the recognition practices, leaders foster a culture of appreciation that's built from the ground up, ensuring its long-term sustainability and a deeper connection between leadership and staff. Recognition has a far-reaching impact, and when embedded deeply into the team culture, it becomes a powerful tool that reinforces a sense of purpose, ownership, and belonging. Those recognized and appreciated for their contributions feel motivated to go the extra mile for the team, knowing their hard work is valued. This builds momentum that drives even greater achievements and fosters a constant cycle of positive engagement and accountability. It establishes an ecosystem where all team members share in the success and learn together from challenges. By continuously shaping a culture of recognition, leaders ensure that team members feel not only appreciated but understood, where every contribution, big or small, is seen as essential to the whole. The ultimate result is a unified and motivated workforce that consistently strives for collective success. Leaders should be mindful of the diversity within their team and make an effort to recognize contributions from all corners of the organization. This might involve being more proactive in seeking out and acknowledging the work of those who might not naturally seek the spotlight, or who might be in roles that are less visible but no less important. By making recognition inclusive, leaders can help to build a more equitable and supportive work environment, where everyone feels valued and appreciated for their contributions. In addition to public recognition, it is also important to ensure that recognition is shared with the broader organization. This might involve sharing stories of recognition in company-wide communications or creating opportunities for team members to be recognized at higher levels of the organization. By doing so, leaders not only reinforce the value of recognition but also help to build a culture of appreciation across the entire organization, where everyone, regardless of their position, feels valued and respected. Recognizing and appreciating everyone within the team is not just a nice-to-have; it is a fundamental part of building a positive, productive, and cohesive work environment. By creating a culture of recognition, personalizing appreciation, encouraging peer-to-peer recognition, recognizing effort as well as outcomes, and making recognition visible and inclusive, leaders can ensure that every team member feels valued and appreciated for their contributions. This culture of recognition not only boosts morale and motivation but also strengthens the bonds between team members, creating a work environment where everyone feels connected, supported, and empowered to do their best work. Ultimately, it is through recognition and appreciation that teams can build the trust, respect, and an engaged team that are essential for long-term success.

TIMOTHY K ELLSWORTH

CULTIVATING CONNECTIONS
Together We Thrive

Creating a culture within a team that fosters a family-like atmosphere leads to a highly engaged and motivated team. However, sustaining this culture over the long term is where the true challenge and reward lie. A family-like culture is characterized by deep trust, mutual support, and a strong sense of belonging among team members. It's a culture where everyone feels valued and connected, not just as colleagues but as part of a close-knit team that genuinely cares about one another. As teams grow, evolve, and face various challenges, maintaining this culture requires intentional effort to ensure it remains strong, adaptable, and aligned with the team's needs. This chapter explores strategies for embedding the family-like culture into the organization's core, adapting it to change, ensuring ongoing leadership commitment, regularly assessing its strength, and celebrating its milestones to keep the culture vibrant and thriving. To effectively embed this culture, leaders need to ensure that all practices and policies within the organization are in harmony with the family-like atmosphere. This could involve revisiting existing policies to ensure they promote inclusivity, fairness, and support for every team member. For instance, policies related to work-life balance, employee well-being, and professional development should be designed to reflect the organization's commitment to caring for its people. Additionally, decision-making processes should be transparent and inclusive, allowing team members to feel involved and respected. By embedding the culture in these foundational elements, leaders create an environment where the family-like atmosphere becomes a natural and consistent part of the team's experience. However, sustaining this culture isn't just about embedding it in the present; it's also about ensuring that it can adapt to future changes and challenges. Teams are dynamic entities that grow and evolve over time, and it's crucial that the culture evolves with them. Whether it's through team expansion, shifts in leadership, or external challenges like economic changes, the culture must be flexible enough to accommodate these changes while staying true to its core values. This adaptability ensures that the culture remains relevant, supportive, and resilient in the face of change. Adapting the culture to change requires foresight and proactive planning. Leaders should anticipate changes and consider how they might impact the team's culture. For instance, when new members join the team, it's important to integrate them into the existing culture while also being open to the fresh perspectives they bring. This might involve updating on-boarding processes to ensure new hires quickly connect with the culture and find their place within the team. By involving the team in these conversations early, leaders reinforce the idea that the culture is a shared responsibility and that everyone has a role in sustaining it over the long term. Ongoing leadership commitment is another essential element in maintaining a family-like culture. Leaders set the tone for the entire organization, and their commitment to nurturing and reinforcing the culture is critical to its longevity. This commitment should be evident in leaders' actions, decisions, and communications, consistently reflecting the values of the family-like culture. Leaders must model the behaviors they wish to see in their team members, demonstrating trust, respect, and support in all interactions. They should also be champions of the culture, actively promoting it and ensuring it is recognized and celebrated within the organization. Leadership commitment also means staying attuned to the evolving needs of the team and continuously reinforcing the culture. Regular check-ins and open forums where team members can discuss the culture, share their experiences, and offer feedback are vital. These conversations allow leaders to gauge the culture's health and make necessary adjustments to keep it aligned with the team's needs. By maintaining an ongoing dialogue about the culture, leaders demonstrate their dedication to sustaining it and adapting it as necessary to support the team's long-term success. Regularly assessing and adjusting the culture is another key strategy for sustaining it over time. Just as an organization's goals and strategies are periodically reviewed and updated, the culture should also be regularly assessed to ensure it remains strong and effective. This can be done through formal assessments, such as surveys or focus groups, as well as informal check-ins and discussions. The aim is to evaluate how well the culture is functioning, identify any areas that may need reinforcement, and take action to address potential issues before they become significant problems. These assessments should be thorough, considering all aspects of the culture, from how well it is integrated into daily practices to how team members perceive and experience it. Leaders should be open to feedback and willing to make changes based on the findings of these assessments. This might involve tweaking policies, introducing new initiatives, or making more substantial changes to ensure the culture remains robust and aligned with the team's evolving needs. By regularly assessing and adjusting the culture, leaders show their commitment to its long-term sustainability and ensure it continues to support the team's engagement and motivation. Creating a true sense of belonging starts with small but powerful gestures that align the core values with practical daily activities. If leaders treat the team as more than a group of workers, but as individuals who matter beyond their professional role, this fosters a culture of mutual care. It's important that this environment includes moments of personal interaction that nurture individual connections, such as learning names, interests, and celebrating life events. These moments don't have to be grand, but they become meaningful when people feel seen and valued for who they are. The environment we create sets the tone for the team's overall culture, making trust an essential ingredient for long-term commitment. Leaders who integrate these small but crucial interpersonal steps into their daily approach exemplify how to lead by caring, demonstrating that the team is more than an organizational structure. It is through these human-centered actions that trust builds a foundation for a lasting family-like atmosphere. The foundation of fostering a culture that mirrors the atmosphere of a close-knit family lies heavily in the decisions leaders make at pivotal moments. Decisions in moments of challenge are the crucibles through which trust is tested. When challenges arise, as they inevitably do, how a leader handles those circumstances is a defining factor in whether or not the cultural integrity is maintained. While all teams will face conflicts, including moments of adversity where opinions clash or unforeseen hurdles appear, it's how these situations are approached that solidify or shake the cultural bond. Leaders should acknowledge the difficulty of the situation and provide consistent support, reinforcing values like collaboration and respect despite setbacks. Additionally, empowering team members to navigate conflicts themselves, as needed, is also an investment in strengthening the culture, allowing personal autonomy while still reinforcing the idea of a collective and unyielding support system. A healthy culture isn't simply set up to be maintained in the most straightforward periods; it's tested during change. Every new introduction to a team dynamic, whether that's new hires, redefined roles, or changing organizational goals, will influence the existing culture. This is where thoughtful leadership comes in, ensuring there is room for inclusivity. Adjusting leadership strategies for new circumstances while keeping an eye on the larger picture and mission of the team's culture provides a resilient foundation. The work involved in ensuring smooth transitions often involves anticipating change before it fully arrives, preparing the team for new priorities and maintaining a narrative that connects back to the central values that ground the team. As new processes, individuals, and challenges emerge, understanding the natural pull of team dynamics will guide leaders in sculpting their approach so that the fabric of the family-like atmosphere remains intact. Continuous improvement means leaders and the team must go beyond adjusting once and expecting the family-like culture to remain self-sustaining. Embedding regular check-ins as part of the ongoing interaction reinforces the emotional connection and sense of belonging over time. These consistent discussions reflect a proactive attitude, allowing leaders to not only check the pulse of how the culture is evolving, but also make space for members to voice their opinions. Healthy cultures thrive on shared ownership, with a recognition that maintaining the culture is not the sole responsibility of leadership, but of everyone within the team. Keeping lines of communication open around the health of the team's culture allows leadership to identify moments of need for an adaptive shift or recognition of growth, preventing any disconnect before it has the chance to grow into a more significant issue. These continuous conversations solidify trust and transparency within the team, making it easier for change to be absorbed harmoniously. It is imperative that team members always see their leaders upholding the cultural tenets they're asked to value. What leaders do speaks volumes over what they say, so reinforcing the desired cultural behaviors through consistent action and embodiment of those values is the surest way to motivate team engagement. The personal commitment of leadership should also encourage team members to live out similar qualities in their interactions with one another. A leader who demonstrates care, humility, and respect for others sets the behavioral standard for the rest of the team, compelling team members to mirror these actions naturally. It's through intentional modeling of trust-building behaviors, open dialogue, and active participation in recognizing achievements that leaders reinforce the idea that a positive and family-like environment is not only beneficial for the organization but vital for everyone's collective success. Maintaining a family-like culture isn't always a passive process, it's something that requires active effort, awareness, and resilience. To sustain this environment through trials, maintaining some routine and ritual that reflects the organization's values helps center a team under duress or unpredictability. These rituals, be they formal moments like team meetings or informal ones such as celebrating milestones or small wins, become the comforting anchor during harder transitions.

They reconnect team members with the collective mission and shared responsibility while helping them see themselves not just as cogs in a machine but as a unified entity with a purpose that transcends the moment. Rituals should also be intentionally reflective of the spirit and identity of the team, using past successes, lessons learned from failure, and shared values to provide opportunities for inspiration even when times are tough. The language that leaders and team members use when speaking about the team itself can reinforce or erode the culture. Using language that emphasizes unity, belonging, and shared ownership provides a solid reinforcement of the family-like atmosphere. Phrases like "we are all in this together," or "this is how we work as a family," communicate inclusion and create consistent reinforcement of cultural values. Additionally, this linguistic consistency needs to extend beyond just leadership, it must be something that all team members embrace and implement within their language and behavior. When all members are reinforcing this same commitment through daily communication, both formal and informal, the idea that the team is built like a family becomes ingrained, creating a stronger, more visible culture of connection. These words and language behaviors support a more inclusive environment, where everyone's contributions are not only heard but respected. Every organization faces a high level of diversity, whether in work styles, personalities, and backgrounds or differing professional motivations and perspectives. As teams grow, the organization is likely to see these diversities challenge the foundational atmosphere of inclusivity unless leaders take steps to weave them into the culture actively. Recognizing the need for nuance and acceptance of the various traits and talents within the team ensures that all members not only feel included but also actively valued for their unique contribution. It's critical that an inclusive environment extends far beyond hiring practices, demanding leadership's commitment to celebrate differences. When differences are celebrated rather than ignored, there is room for open and constructive dialogue, creativity, and adaptability, creating a climate where diverse ways of thinking add more depth to the family-like atmosphere. Resilience in any work culture stems from how well the team responds to obstacles and uncertainty. A family-like culture should empower individuals to face challenges head-on, knowing that they are supported emotionally and professionally. When setbacks occur, be it in individual performance or as a team, the response from leadership has the power to influence whether those obstacles feel insurmountable or simply part of the team's collective learning. Maintaining an unwavering support system even during difficult times creates a safe environment for reflection, personal growth, and productivity. It ensures that challenges remain opportunities to grow stronger as a team, not as separations between individual achievements. Leaders should teach by example that resilience isn't about brushing off adversity but leaning into it as a group, learning from it, and emerging more connected than ever. Celebrating the team's culture, not just the outcomes, is a key ingredient in promoting long-term success. Frequently taking a moment to celebrate the victories that represent the strength of the culture, whether it's overcoming obstacles, supporting a team member through a difficult time, or demonstrating unity in decision-making, helps bring focus back to the cultural accomplishments rather than just productivity. These moments allow team members to recognize that the fabric of their collective actions is what holds everything together, creating a sense of ownership that fuels future growth. Acknowledging cultural milestones is a reminder that the company's commitment to fostering a team that feels as close as family is as valuable as any other business achievement. Celebrating cultural milestones is another powerful way to sustain a family-like culture over the long term. Just as teams celebrate project completions and personal achievements, it's important to recognize and celebrate the longevity and success of the culture itself. These celebrations serve as a reminder of the progress the team has made, the challenges they've overcome, and the values that have guided them. They also reinforce the significance of the culture, reminding team members that it is something to be cherished and nurtured. Cultural milestones could include anniversaries of the culture's establishment, significant achievements that reflect the culture's values, or moments when the culture was especially evident in the team's actions. These milestones should be celebrated in a way that reflects the team's unique identity, whether through formal ceremonies, informal gatherings, or creative expressions like storytelling or art. The goal is to make these celebrations meaningful and inclusive, ensuring that everyone feels connected to and proud of the culture they've helped build. Sustaining a family-like culture over the long term requires a deliberate and multifaceted approach. It involves embedding the culture deeply into the organization's practices, adapting it to meet new challenges, ensuring ongoing leadership commitment, regularly assessing its strength, and celebrating its milestones. By taking these steps, leaders can create a work environment where the family-like culture not only endures but thrives, continuing to engage and motivate the team for years to come. This culture, characterized by trust, support, and mutual respect, becomes the foundation upon which long-term success is built, allowing the team to navigate challenges, seize opportunities, and achieve lasting fulfillment together. When each member feels secure in their role and valued within the larger framework of the team, they are more willing to push the boundaries of their potential, stepping into new challenges with confidence. This supportive environment promotes innovation and creative problem-solving, as team members are encouraged to contribute their unique ideas and perspectives without fear of judgment. Moreover, as obstacles arise, the cohesive nature of the culture ensures the team faces them as a united front, strengthening bonds and resilience. By continuously upholding the values of trust and mutual respect, team members cultivate a deep sense of shared purpose that allows them to focus on their collective goals. Ultimately, this alignment propels the team toward not just professional accomplishments, but a deeper fulfillment that comes from being part of something greater than themselves, creating an enduring legacy of success that is built on a foundation of shared values, support, and a commitment to one another's growth.

TIMOTHY K ELLSWORTH

STRONGER BONDS
Better Outcomes

Relationships are the backbone of any thriving culture, and I've seen firsthand how they can make or break the success of a team. Strong connections between leaders and team members form the foundation for mutual respect, cooperation, and shared purpose. It's not just about working together; it's about building bridges that break down walls, whether those walls are created by hierarchy, job roles, or even personal insecurities. To build these connections, leaders must intentionally step into the role of relationship builders, showing up as authentic, approachable, and genuinely interested in their team members' lives and experiences. In my own experience, the smallest gestures often have the biggest impact. A handshake that lingers with intention, a heartfelt conversation about someone's weekend, or a genuine "How are you?" can lead to significant shifts in how team members feel valued. These seemingly simple actions create ripple effects, showing that leadership cares not just about the results but about the people achieving them. Each interaction is a touchpoint for reinforcing the shared goals and vision of the team, reminding everyone why they show up every day. Building meaningful connections isn't limited to one-on-one interactions. It's Equally important to bridge the gaps between departments. I've encountered situations where interdepartmental silos created unnecessary barriers, reducing both productivity and morale. When leaders encourage collaboration across teams, they break down these silos, fostering a sense of unity that enhances innovation and efficiency. It's about creating an environment where the left hand knows what the right hand is doing, and everyone feels they are rowing in the same direction. Meaningful relationships also require a degree of vulnerability, a lesson I've learned through personal growth and mistakes. Leaders who are willing to admit when they're wrong, ask for help, or seek advice from their team members set the tone for a culture of mutual respect and growth. When leaders model humility, they create an atmosphere where team members feel safe to express their own ideas, take risks, and grow professionally. This openness transforms the leader-follower dynamic into a partnership, with everyone working together to achieve success. One of the most remarkable outcomes of strong connections is the boost in morale they provide. When team members feel genuinely appreciated and seen, they are more likely to go above and beyond for the organization. I've witnessed how small, consistent acts of appreciation can turn disengaged individuals into enthusiastic contributors. This sense of being valued isn't just a morale booster; it's a powerful motivator that drives teams to achieve results they didn't think possible. However, building relationships in the workplace isn't without its challenges. Striking the right balance between professional boundaries and authentic personal engagement is essential. While relationships rooted in care and connection can strengthen teams, it's crucial to maintain a level of professionalism that ensures respect and focus on organizational goals. Navigating this balance has taught me that relationships are about more than just camaraderie; they're about creating a community where every individual feels they belong while still being held accountable to shared standards. Relationships aren't an afterthought or an accessory to workplace culture; they are the culture. Without them, the workplace becomes mechanical and transactional, a place where people merely clock in and out without a sense of purpose. Strong connections infuse humanity into every aspect of daily operations, making the workplace feel alive and meaningful. When leaders prioritize relationships, they create a culture that doesn't just survive but thrives, drawing out the best in everyone and inspiring loyalty, collaboration, and a shared commitment to success. Integrity forms the bedrock of every successful relationship in the workplace. Without it, connections remain superficial and transactional, incapable of weathering challenges or fostering genuine collaboration.

Integrity begins when leaders align their words and actions, showing consistency in every decision they make. This alignment sets the tone for an honest and dependable culture. When team members see their leaders living out the values they preach, trust grows organically, creating a foundation for deeper, more meaningful relationships. In my own experience, I've learned that no connection thrives where trust is absent, and trust simply cannot exist without integrity. Demonstrating integrity starts with transparency. Sharing the "why" behind decisions, especially difficult ones, helps team members feel included and valued. I've often found that when leaders open-up about their reasoning, even unpopular choices are met with greater understanding and acceptance. Transparency also reduces the potential for misunderstandings, ensuring that team members remain aligned with leadership goals. This practice turns decision-making into a shared journey, one where everyone feels their perspective matters and that they're part of the bigger picture. Trust is further strengthened when team members are actively involved in problem-solving. Leaders who impose solutions without consultation risk alienating their teams, while those who collaborate foster unity. I've seen how involving team members in tackling challenges encourages a sense of ownership and commitment. This approach not only builds trust but also leads to innovative solutions that might not emerge from a single perspective. Collaboration rooted in integrity ensures that no one feels overlooked or undervalued. Integrity truly shines in the face of mistakes or setbacks. Leaders who approach errors with honesty and accountability set an example for their teams. I've found that when mistakes are handled openly and with sincerity, respect is preserved, and trust is often strengthened. Team members are far more forgiving of missteps when they see that leadership's intentions are fair and rooted in a genuine desire to grow. This kind of integrity fosters resilience within relationships, ensuring they remain intact even during challenging times. Recognizing and celebrating achievements is another vital expression of integrity. When leaders give credit where it's due, they show that they value the contributions of their team members. I've seen how acknowledging both large accomplishments and everyday efforts inspires loyalty and deepens connections. By genuinely celebrating individual and collective successes, leaders demonstrate that they're paying attention and that every contribution matters. This recognition strengthens bonds and cultivates a sense of shared pride across the team. Authenticity plays a crucial role in building trust through integrity. Leaders who are honest about their strengths, weaknesses, and intentions foster an environment where team members feel safe to do the same. I've always found that when people are free to bring their authentic selves to work, it strengthens relationships and nurtures a sense of belonging. Authenticity breaks down pretenses and encourages open, honest communication, which is essential for creating a thriving team culture rooted in mutual respect. Consistency is perhaps the most critical aspect of integrity. Favouritism or the inconsistent application of rules erodes trust and creates division. I've learned that fairness ensures every team member feels Equally valued, reinforcing the relationships that bind the team together. Integrity demands that leaders remain steady in their principles, treating everyone with the same level of respect and accountability. This consistency transforms relationships from being merely transactional to becoming deeply transformative. At its core, integrity aligns individual and collective goals, turning workplace connections into powerful forces for growth. It's not just about creating a trustworthy culture; it's about inspiring a sense of purpose that motivates everyone to give their best. When integrity is upheld, relationships thrive, and teams evolve into supportive, high-performing communities where trust, respect, and authenticity fuel lasting success. Trust is the cornerstone of all successful relationships. Without it, even the best-intentioned leadership strategies fail to gain traction. From my experience, I've seen that trust is not something that can be demanded; it must be earned through consistent and deliberate actions. Cultivating trust requires more than just good intentions, it demands reliability, integrity, and unwavering commitment. When team members trust their leaders, they are willing to invest their energy and creativity, knowing they are in a safe and dependable environment. Trust doesn't just build relationships; it lays the foundation for a thriving culture. One of the most effective ways to foster trust is through competence. Leaders who demonstrate mastery of their roles instill confidence in their teams. Making sound decisions, providing clear direction, and consistently delivering results reassures team members that they are in capable hands. I've always found that when leaders act decisively and with expertise, it sends a powerful message: "You can count on me." This competence fosters respect, strengthens bonds, and creates a culture where team members feel secure in their roles. Vulnerability is another vital aspect of trust. Leaders who are open about their challenges, struggles, and uncertainties humanize themselves, making it easier for team members to relate to them. I've learned that being honest about what you don't know and inviting collaboration strengthens the connection between leaders and their teams. Vulnerability isn't a weakness; it's a bridge to mutual understanding. When leaders and team members support one another during difficult times, they form unbreakable bonds rooted in empathy and shared purpose. Follow-through is essential to maintaining trust. Nothing erodes confidence faster than broken promises or unmet expectations. I've seen how damaging it can be when leaders fail to deliver on their commitments, leaving team members feeling disillusioned and hesitant to rely on them. Trust requires consistency, leaders must align their actions with their words, reinforcing reliability at every turn. When promises are kept, team members know they can depend on their leaders, creating an environment of mutual respect and accountability. Communication is the glue that holds trust together. Keeping team members informed fosters a sense of inclusion and alignment. I've found that transparency is especially critical during times of uncertainty or change. Sharing updates about progress, challenges, and decisions, even when the news isn't positive, helps maintain trust by showing that leaders are not hiding anything. Open communication builds bridges, ensuring that team members feel connected to the larger goals and understand their role in achieving them. Rebuilding trust after it has been broken is one of the greatest leadership challenges, but it's not impossible. Addressing issues directly, apologizing sincerely, and committing to change can begin the process of repair. I've seen firsthand how leaders who take accountability for their mistakes earn renewed respect from their teams. Rebuilding trust takes time and effort, requiring consistent actions that demonstrate a genuine desire to make things right. While the journey may be difficult, the rewards of restored trust are immeasurable, leading to stronger and more resilient relationships. When trust flourishes, collaboration becomes second nature. Team members are more willing to share ideas, take risks, and support one another. Trust is the ultimate enabler of collective success. It transforms a group of individuals into a cohesive, high-performing team. A culture of trust creates an environment where relationships deepen, innovation thrives, and everyone feels valued. By prioritizing trust, leaders not only strengthen relationships but also unlock the full potential of their teams, paving the way for long-term success. Trust is not a one-time achievement, it's an ongoing commitment. It requires constant nurturing through actions, communication, and accountability. Leaders who prioritize trust build bridges that connect people, departments, and goals, creating a thriving workplace where relationships and performance reach new heights. When trust becomes the foundation of an organization, it fosters a culture of confidence, collaboration, and shared success. Emotional intelligence is a cornerstone of meaningful leadership and is indispensable in building strong, lasting relationships. It's not just about managing emotions, it's about understanding how emotions drive behaviour and decisions. Leaders who are emotionally intelligent create an environment where team members feel heard, valued, and supported. Emotional intelligence isn't just a tool; it's a bridge that connects people, creating bonds rooted in understanding and empathy. In every interaction, it reminds us that we are dealing with people, not just tasks or roles. One of the most vital aspects of emotional intelligence is empathy. Recognizing and validating the emotions of team members builds trust and loyalty. I've seen how simply listening to someone's concerns or acknowledging their challenges can shift the dynamic of a conversation from transactional to transformational. Empathy goes beyond words; it's about genuinely stepping into someone else's shoes and showing that their experiences matter. This approach fosters a sense of belonging and demonstrates that leaders care about more than just performance metrics. Active listening is another critical element of emotional intelligence. It's not just about hearing what someone says but about truly understanding the message behind the words. In my experience, leaders who listen attentively can uncover the root causes of issues before they escalate. By picking up on non-verbal cues, such as body language and tone, leaders can respond with greater sensitivity. This practice not only diffuses potential conflicts but also strengthens relationships by showing team members they have a voice that matters. Emotional intelligence also involves a deep level of self-awareness. Leaders who understand how their actions and words affect others are better Equipped to maintain harmony within their teams. I've learned that a well-timed pause or a shift in tone can make all the difference in how a message is received. Self-awareness isn't just about knowing your strengths and weaknesses; it's about recognizing the emotional impact you have on others and adjusting accordingly. This adaptability fosters respect and strengthens connections. Building emotional intelligence is a journey that requires intention, practice, and feedback. I've found that seeking input from team members is one of the most effective ways to refine relational skills. Asking questions like, "How could I have handled that better?" opens the door to growth and demonstrates humility. Regularly engaging in self-reflection and soliciting constructive feedback helps leaders identify blind spots and improve their interactions. Developing emotional intelligence is not about perfection but progress, as every effort contributes to stronger relationships. Emotional intelligence doesn't just benefit individual relationships, it shapes the culture of an organization. When leaders prioritize understanding and compassion, they set a standard for how team members interact with one another. I've seen how a culture rooted in emotional intelligence encourages open communication, collaboration, and constructive conflict resolution. It creates an atmosphere where people feel safe to express themselves, share ideas, and work together towards common goals. This dynamic not only enhances team performance but also makes the workplace more fulfilling and enjoyable for everyone. The true power of emotional intelligence lies in its ability to humanize leadership. It bridges the gap between logic and compassion, balancing the drive for results with genuine care for people. Leaders who prioritize emotional intelligence inspire greater commitment to shared goals because team members feel valued as individuals. Emotional intelligence is not just a skill, it's a mindset that transforms relationships and cultures. When leaders lead with emotional intelligence, they don't just build teams; they build communities where trust, respect, and connection thrive. Emotional intelligence is the thread that weaves together effective leadership and meaningful relationships. It's not a one-time achievement but an ongoing practice that requires dedication and awareness. Leaders who embrace emotional intelligence create a culture of understanding, compassion, and collaboration, fostering an environment where everyone can thrive. Silos are one of the most stubborn challenges in any organization, and they are far more than just physical barriers. Whether operational or emotional, silos create separation that stifles collaboration and innovation. Relationships within teams are critical, but unless we intentionally build interdepartmental connections, these silos will persist, leading to inefficiencies and misunderstandings. Dismantling silos isn't just a task, it's a mindset. It begins with fostering relationships that span departments, breaking the walls that divide us and building bridges that unite us. Breaking silos starts with creating opportunities for cross-departmental engagement. I've found that regular team-building activities, joint projects, or even informal gatherings can help team members get to know each other beyond their job titles. When people connect as individuals, they begin to see the value in each other's contributions. Leaders must actively support these initiatives, modelling a commitment to collaboration. These efforts don't just improve workflow; they humanize the workplace, transforming teams into a unified organization. Encouraging a culture of transparency is another vital step. Team members often operate in isolation because they don't understand how their work fits into the bigger picture. I've seen how providing visibility into the roles and contributions of different departments can change this dynamic. When people understand how their efforts connect to the organization's mission and goals, they develop a shared sense of purpose. Transparency breaks down the "us vs. them" mentality and replaces it with a spirit of collective achievement. Communication plays a pivotal role in breaking silos. It needs to be intentional, frequents, and meaningful. Regular cross-departmental check-ins or collaborative planning sessions allow team members to share updates, align their efforts, and build trust. These meetings are more than just a logistical necessity, they're an opportunity to foster camaraderie. Leaders like me need to facilitate these interactions, ensuring they are productive but also personal, reinforcing the importance of mutual respect and understanding. Conflict is often at the heart of silos, typically stemming from misunderstandings or misaligned priorities. I've learned that when these conflicts arise, it's essential to mediate with empathy. By focusing on solutions that benefit all parties, leaders can turn tension into opportunities for growth. Encouraging team members to walk in each other's shoes, whether through role shadowing or joint problem-solving exercises, deepens interdepartmental relationships and cultivates mutual understanding. Celebrating wins as an organization, rather than attributing success to individual teams, is a powerful way to dismantle silos. I make it a point to highlight cross-departmental efforts during celebrations and acknowledge the collective contributions of everyone involved. This practice reinforces the idea that success is a shared accomplishment. By emphasizing shared accountability, leaders can build a culture where collaboration is not just encouraged, it becomes second nature. Breaking silos is about more than improving communication or efficiency; it's about creating a unified entity. When silos are dismantled, the organization becomes a thriving ecosystem where every department supports the others. I've seen firsthand how this unity leads to greater innovation, higher morale, and a more cohesive culture. Team members feel connected not just to their immediate peers but to the organization. This sense of belonging energizes the entire team, driving success on every level. From my experience, breaking silos isn't easy, but it's essential for creating a culture where relationships, collaboration, and innovation thrive. By fostering transparency, promoting shared accountability, and facilitating meaningful connections between departments, leaders can transform their organizations into cohesive, efficient, and resilient entities. When we break down the barriers that divide us, we unlock the potential of our people, enabling them to achieve extraordinary results together. Building strong workplace relationships requires a delicate balance between connection and professionalism. While fostering meaningful personal connections can drive collaboration and morale, clear boundaries must be maintained to ensure relationships remain respectful, equitable, and productive. This balance is not an obstacle but an opportunity to create a thriving culture of trust and professionalism. It is up to leaders, including myself, to model this balance effectively, demonstrating how to engage with empathy and authenticity while maintaining the professionalism necessary for fair and objective decision-making. Leaders must set the tone for maintaining professional boundaries. In my experience, it starts with self-awareness and clear communication. Whether through everyday interactions or high-stakes decisions, we need to avoid favouritism or any behaviour that could appear to compromise fairness. Consistency is key.

Team members should see that personal connections never cloud professional judgement. By demonstrating this consistently, I ensure that respect remains the foundation of all workplace interactions, creating an environment where fairness is not just a value but a lived reality. Empathy plays a vital role in workplace relationships, but it must always be paired with respect for individual privacy. I've learned to walk the fine line between caring and overstepping, ensuring that my support doesn't invade personal territories. For example, while I make an effort to understand my team members' challenges and show care, I also respect when they prefer to keep certain aspects of their lives private. By allowing people to set their own boundaries, I foster trust and create an environment where team members feel safe and respected. Communication is a cornerstone of balancing boundaries. I prioritize open dialogue about expectations, making it clear that while personal connections are valued, professionalism must always come first. Regular conversations help reinforce this balance, ensuring everyone understands the role of boundaries in creating a harmonious workplace. These discussions also empower team members to voice their comfort levels, fostering mutual respect. By encouraging this level of communication, I've found that the entire team becomes more mindful of how they interact, ensuring that relationships enhance, rather than detract from, the workplace culture. Addressing conflict is another area where balancing boundaries is crucial. I've faced situations where personal relationships within the team complicated conflicts, making resolution more challenging. To mediate effectively, I focus on the facts and remain impartial. By avoiding personal biases and addressing issues with fairness and transparency, I ensure that relationships are preserved even as conflicts are resolved. This approach not only resolves disputes but also strengthens trust, showing the team that professionalism always guides my decisions. Reinforcing the importance of mutual respect is an ongoing effort. I consistently remind my team that while personal connections are valuable, they must be grounded in respect for each other's boundaries. Regular team discussions or workshops on workplace dynamics can reinforce these principles, providing a shared understanding of how to balance empathy with professionalism. These initiatives encourage team members to support each other without overstepping, creating a culture of collaboration that respects individuality and diversity. Striking this balance ultimately ensures that workplace relationships remain a source of strength rather than a point of contention. I've seen how clear boundaries create a culture where people feel safe to engage, collaborate, and contribute without fear of overreach or bias. By modelling this balance and embedding it into the team's culture, I've been able to foster an environment where personal connections enhance our collective success without compromising the professionalism that drives it. It's a responsibility that starts with leadership and extends to every team member. When boundaries are respected and upheld, trust flourishes, morale rises, and the team operates at its best. This balance is the foundation of a culture that values both the humanity of its people and the excellence of its outcomes. Building strong workplace relationships requires deliberate and ongoing investment. Relationships, much like anything of true value, demand consistent care, time, and effort to thrive. I have learned that the more intentional I am about nurturing these connections, the stronger the bonds become, leading to a culture grounded in trust, respect, and loyalty. Investing in relationships isn't just a task, it's a mindset, a commitment to prioritizing people above processes and fostering a workplace where everyone feels genuinely valued. My approach to investing in relationships begins with one-on-one interactions. I make it a point to connect personally with each team member, learning about their strengths, challenges, and aspirations. These conversations are not superficial. they provide me with invaluable insights into how I can better support and guide them. Whether it's offering encouragement during a tough project or celebrating a personal milestone, these moments of connection reinforce to my team members that they matter as individuals, not just contributors to organizational goals. Investing in team dynamics is Equally important. I've organized team-building activities and facilitated open dialogues to create opportunities for collaboration and camaraderie. These shared experiences break down barriers, strengthen bonds, and help foster a sense of unity within the group. Celebrating milestones, both big and small, is another way I cultivate these connections. Acknowledging birthdays, project completions, or even personal achievements builds a sense of community that extends beyond the workplace. One of the most impactful ways I've invested in relationships is by prioritizing professional development. Supporting my team members' growth, whether through training, mentorship, or stretch assignments, shows them that I care about their success beyond their current roles. I know that when I invest in their future, they feel valued and are more likely to give their best to the team. This reciprocal relationship of investment and dedication creates a cycle of loyalty and motivation that benefits everyone. Recognizing individual contributions is another cornerstone of my relationship-building efforts. Simple gestures, like a heartfelt thank-you or public acknowledgment of someone's efforts, go a long way in making team members feel appreciated. These acts of gratitude, while small, carry immense weight in showing my team that I see and value their hard work. They also inspire others to celebrate each other's successes, fostering a positive and supportive team culture. Challenges are inevitable in any relationship, and I've learned the importance of addressing them proactively and constructively. When conflicts arise, I approach them with care, aiming to understand all perspectives before working toward a resolution. These moments, while difficult, often become opportunities to deepen trust and strengthen relationships. By handling challenges with integrity and empathy, I demonstrate my commitment to preserving and growing these connections, even in tough times. Over time, I've seen firsthand how these investments pay dividends. A cohesive, motivated, and engaged team doesn't happen by chance. It's the result of consistent effort, genuine care, and a shared commitment to nurturing relationships. The bonds we build create a culture where team members feel connected not only to each other but also to the organization's success. This sense of connection drives collaboration, innovation, and a deep sense of purpose that benefits everyone involved. Investing in relationships is, at its core, about prioritizing people. By consistently dedicating time and energy to fostering connections, I've been able to create an environment where trust and loyalty thrive. Relationships are the heartbeat of any thriving culture, and by valuing them as such, I've seen my team flourish, not just as professionals but as people. This commitment to nurturing relationships is one of the most rewarding aspects of leadership, and it continues to inspire me every day. Relationships are truly the lifeblood of a thriving culture. Without them, even the most well-crafted strategy, vision, or mission will inevitably fall short. Over the years, I've learned that the heart of leadership lies in building connections rooted in authenticity, integrity, and trust. This chapter reflects that journey, highlighting how these elements shape not only individual interactions but the entire dynamic of a team or organization. Whether it's breaking silos, maintaining balanced boundaries, or investing in personal and collective growth, each aspect plays a vital role in cultivating an environment where relationships can flourish. For me, relationships go beyond professional obligations. They are a reflection of the organization's true values and vision. I've seen firsthand how leaders, myself included, have the power to nurture these connections by showing empathy, practicing emotional intelligence, and demonstrating consistent care. When team members feel genuinely seen, heard, and valued, something remarkable happens. They become more engaged, loyal, and collaborative, forging a shared commitment to success. Relationships also bridge the gaps that might otherwise separate individuals or departments. I've experienced the power of uniting people under a common purpose, watching barriers dissolve and camaraderie grow. These bonds don't just strengthen the workplace, they build resilience and drive innovation. Every day presents opportunities to deepen these connections. A simple conversation, a moment of shared understanding, or an expression of appreciation can leave lasting impressions that shape the culture for the better. Moving forward, I remind myself that relationships require daily investment. They thrive on intention and care, and they grow stronger when nurtured consistently. I view every interaction as a chance to reinforce the values that define a thriving culture, trust, respect, and collaboration. By investing in these connections, I believe we create not only a foundation for success but a team capable of achieving greatness together. In the end, relationships are what truly drive the success of any organization. They inspire us to be better, to work harder, and to stay resilient in the face of challenges. As a leader, I am committed to making these bonds a priority every day, knowing that they are the key to creating a united, dynamic, and thriving culture. Together, through these relationships, we can achieve more than we ever could alone.

TIMOTHY K ELLSWORTH

EMOTIONAL INTELLIGENCE
The Power Within

Emotional intelligence (EI) is the unseen driver of successful leadership, the force that turns strategy into reality and vision into action. While technical skills and expertise are crucial, EI is what enables leaders to connect with their teams on a deeper level, creating bonds that inspire collaboration and commitment. From my experience, I've found that understanding the emotions of others and managing my own is not just a helpful tool but the cornerstone of effective leadership. Leadership isn't just about achieving objectives; it's about bringing out the best in people, and EI makes that possible. Teams thrive when their leaders demonstrate empathy, self-awareness, and emotional regulation. I've seen how an emotionally intelligent leader can transform a room, defusing tensions and building bridges between individuals with different perspectives. In logistics, where timelines are tight and pressure can mount quickly, this ability is invaluable. A leader with EI doesn't just manage workflows but also understands the dynamics and emotions of their team, creating an environment where challenges become opportunities for growth. Emotional intelligence isn't innate; it's developed through reflection, learning, and intentional practice. For me, this realization came after years of focusing solely on results. Early in my career, I believed that hitting targets was all that mattered. Yet I learned that success built solely on metrics can crumble under the strain of unresolved emotional undercurrents and disengaged team members. Teams are made up of individuals, each with unique strengths, fears, and motivations, and ignoring this truth is a recipe for burnout and turnover. Leadership grounded in EI transforms the workplace from a transactional environment into a vibrant, human-centred culture. When leaders actively listen and respond with empathy, they cultivate trust and loyalty. I've seen team members go above and beyond not because they were told to, but because they felt understood, valued, and supported. This is the kind of engagement that makes a team resilient and adaptable, even in the face of unforeseen challenges. Without EI, leadership can feel cold and detached, like a machine that only cares about output. This approach leads to miscommunication, disengagement, and even resentment. In contrast, emotionally intelligent leaders bring humanity into every interaction. They acknowledge emotions as a vital part of the workplace, addressing frustrations, celebrating successes, and providing support during difficulties. I've learned that when team members feel seen and heard, their dedication and innovation flourish naturally. In logistics, where precision and efficiency are key, the importance of EI is magnified. High-pressure environments often bring out stress and conflict, but emotionally intelligent leadership can turn these moments into opportunities for connection and growth. When I've taken the time to understand the emotions behind a delay or miscommunication, I've often uncovered solutions that not only resolved the issue but also strengthened the team. This kind of leadership fosters an atmosphere of mutual respect and collaboration, where team members feel empowered to share ideas and solve problems together. Emotional intelligence isn't just about being "nice"; it's about being real, present, and purposeful. It's about creating a foundation for long-term success, where relationships and results go hand in hand. In my experience, cultivating EI has been an ongoing journey, one that has deepened my ability to lead and to connect with others. It's the heartbeat of leadership, the unifying force that drives teams to excel. Leadership without EI is hollow, but with it, there's no limit to what a team can achieve together. Emotional intelligence is the backbone of effective leadership, something I've come to understand deeply in my journey as a mentor and coach. While technical skills and strategic thinking are important, they are only part of the equation. True leadership requires the ability to connect with others on a meaningful level, and that starts with mastering the five key components of emotional intelligence: self-awareness, self-regulation, motivation, empathy, and social skills. These aren't abstract ideas, but practical skills that I've seen transform how leaders engage with their teams and navigate challenges. Self-awareness is the cornerstone of emotional intelligence. It begins with the ability to recognize and understand our own emotions, not just on the surface but in their deeper implications. In my leadership experiences, I've learned that being self-aware helps me identify my emotional triggers and recognize patterns in my behaviour. It's about taking the time to reflect and understand what drives reactions, both positive and negative. Self-awareness allows leaders to bring their whole, authentic selves to the table, fostering genuine relationships with their teams. Self-awareness also involves embracing strengths and acknowledging limitations. No leader is perfect, and recognizing where growth is needed is a sign of strength, not weakness. When I became more aware of my own blind spots, I found opportunities for growth and sought feedback to fill those gaps. This humility not only enhances self-awareness but also builds trust within the team. They see a leader willing to learn and grow alongside them. Self-awareness is about understanding the ripple effect of our emotions on others. When I'm frustrated or stressed, I know my team can feel it, even if I don't say a word. Recognizing this impact has taught me to pause, recalibrate, and approach situations with mindfulness. It's not about suppressing emotions but about managing them thoughtfully. This practice sets the tone for how the entire team approaches challenges. Self-regulation builds on the foundation of self-awareness, empowering leaders to control their impulses and respond thoughtfully. In the fast-paced world of logistics, there's no shortage of high-pressure situations. I've learned that the ability to pause and think before acting can mean the difference between escalating a conflict and resolving it productively. Self-regulation is about maintaining composure and professionalism, even in the face of setbacks or frustration. One of the hardest lessons I've learned about self-regulation is the importance of practising patience. When timelines are tight, and tensions are high, it's easy to react impulsively. However, taking a step back and approaching challenges calmly has consistently led to better outcomes. This approach not only defuses tension but also models a sense of stability for the team, inspiring them to handle pressure with the same level-headedness. Another key aspect of self-regulation is adaptability. In logistics, plans can change in an instant, and being able to pivot without losing focus is critical. Leaders who self-regulate effectively can adjust to shifting circumstances with confidence and optimism, ensuring their teams remain motivated and solutions oriented. This adaptability builds resilience, creating a team culture that thrives under uncertainty. Motivation is the inner drive that propels leaders to achieve goals and inspire others. For me, it's never been just about checking items off a to-do list. It's about cultivating a sense of purpose and showing others the value of their contributions. Motivation starts with the leader. When I show passion and determination, my team mirrors that energy, creating a ripple effect that fuels collaboration and innovation. Motivation also means maintaining focus in the face of obstacles. I've faced many moments where plans didn't work out or where challenges seemed insurmountable. In those times, staying motivated required tapping into a vision of what could be achieved and sharing that vision with the team. It's about showing them the bigger picture and reminding them why their work matters. Motivation requires a commitment to personal growth and continuous improvement. As a leader, I'm constantly seeking ways to refine my skills and knowledge. This commitment not only enhances my leadership abilities but also inspires my team members to pursue their own development. A motivated team is one that thrives, driven by a shared commitment to excellence. Empathy is perhaps the most powerful of the five components, allowing leaders to truly understand and connect with their teams. In my experience, empathy isn't just about listening; it's about hearing the unspoken and valuing the emotions behind the words. By putting myself in the shoes of my team members, I can better understand their challenges and motivations. This connection fosters trust and loyalty, creating a foundation for meaningful relationships. Empathy also plays a crucial role in decision-making. When I consider how decisions impact individuals, I'm better equipped to make choices that balance team needs with organisational goals. This doesn't mean avoiding tough decisions but approaching them with compassion and transparency. Empathy ensures that even difficult conversations are handled with care and respect. Empathy transforms the way conflicts are resolved. When disagreements arise, understanding each perspective helps find common ground and build solutions that everyone can support. Empathy doesn't mean avoiding conflict; it means navigating it in a way that strengthens relationships rather than damaging them. Social skills are the glue that ties emotional intelligence together, turning individual components into effective leadership. Strong communication is at the heart of social skills. It's not just about conveying information but doing so in a way that resonates and inspires. Active listening has been a game-changer for me, showing my team that their voices matter and encouraging open dialogue. Social skills also involve the ability to build and maintain relationships across diverse teams. In logistics, where coordination is key, fostering collaboration between departments is essential. By cultivating positive relationships, I've been able to break down silos and create a more cohesive, unified team. Another vital aspect of social skills is conflict resolution. When tensions arise, addressing them directly yet diplomatically ensures that issues are resolved constructively. Leaders with strong social skills don't shy away from difficult conversations; they embrace them as opportunities to strengthen the team. Mastering these five pillars of emotional intelligence has reshaped the way I approach leadership. They've taught me that leading isn't just about achieving results but about building relationships, fostering trust, and creating a culture where everyone can thrive. Emotional intelligence is more than a skill; it's a mindset that transforms challenges into opportunities and creates lasting success. Mastering self-awareness and self-regulation has been one of the most transformative aspects of my leadership journey.

These twin pillars of emotional intelligence are not just abstract concepts; they are the bedrock upon which effective leadership is built. For me, self-awareness began with an honest look at how my emotions impacted my behaviour and, in turn, my team. It was humbling to realize that moments of stress or frustration didn't just stay with me, they rippled out, affecting morale, productivity, and even trust. This understanding marked the beginning of a commitment to lead with intention rather than being driven by unchecked emotion. Self-awareness is about more than just understanding emotions; it's about recognizing their patterns and triggers. Over time, I've noticed how certain situations or pressures tend to provoke specific reactions. For instance, tight deadlines might spark impatience, while unexpected changes could lead to frustration. By identifying these patterns, I've been able to prepare myself mentally, ensuring my responses align with the values I want to model. This intentional approach has helped me maintain a sense of consistency that my team can rely on, even in challenging circumstances. Beyond internal recognition, self-awareness requires an openness to external perspectives. Seeking feedback from colleagues and team members has been invaluable in uncovering blind spots in my leadership. Initially, it wasn't easy to hear critiques about how my actions might have been perceived, but over time, I came to see feedback as a gift rather than a threat. Listening to others' insights has not only deepened my self-awareness but also strengthened trust within the team. They know their perspectives are valued, which fosters a culture of openness and mutual growth. Self-regulation, the natural partner to self-awareness, is the ability to manage those emotions and behaviours effectively. For me, this means pausing before reacting, especially in moments of tension. Early in my career, I learned the hard way that impulsive responses could escalate situations unnecessarily. By practising restraint and choosing my words carefully, I've been able to turn potentially volatile moments into opportunities for constructive dialogue. This skill has been particularly critical in logistics, where high-pressure scenarios are the norm, and calm leadership sets the tone for the entire team. One of the most valuable lessons in self-regulation has been understanding the power of patience. Whether it's waiting for the right time to address a sensitive issue or giving team members the space they need to find solutions, patience often leads to better outcomes than immediate action. Cultivating patience has required intentional effort, but it has paid off in creating a more supportive and collaborative environment. Team members appreciate a leader who doesn't rush to judgment but instead approaches challenges thoughtfully and with an open mind. Self-regulation also extends to maintaining adaptability in the face of change. In the dynamic world of logistics, plans can shift with little notice, and the ability to pivot without losing focus is essential. I've learned that by staying calm and solution oriented, I can help my team navigate uncertainty with confidence. This adaptability not only keeps projects on track but also reinforces a culture of resilience, where challenges are seen as opportunities rather than setbacks. Perhaps most importantly, self-awareness and self-regulation model accountability. As a leader, I've come to see that owning my emotions and actions sets the standard for the team. When I admit mistakes or acknowledge when my emotions have impacted decisions, it creates a culture where others feel safe doing the same. This transparency builds trust and fosters an environment where growth is prioritized over perfection. Ultimately, mastering self-awareness and self-regulation isn't just about managing myself, it's about empowering those around me to thrive in a culture of integrity and understanding. Empathy has become a pillar of my leadership approach, an essential quality that shapes my interactions and decision-making. In my experience, empathy isn't just an add-on; it's a core element that underpins every successful leader's ability to connect and inspire. It allows me to understand not just what my team members are doing but why they are doing it and how they feel in the process. By stepping into their shoes, I can see challenges through their eyes, fostering a sense of solidarity that transforms the dynamic between leader and team into a true partnership. What makes empathy powerful in leadership is its ability to create an atmosphere of trust and understanding. I've learned that when people feel genuinely heard, they are more likely to share openly, whether it's about personal struggles, workplace challenges, or innovative ideas. This open communication strengthens relationships and leads to better problem-solving. For me, taking the time to truly listen, without interrupting or jumping to conclusions, has been one of the most effective ways to show empathy. It's about being present in the moment and demonstrating through action that I value their input. Empathy has also become a critical tool in resolving conflicts, which are inevitable in any fast-paced environment. I've found that approaching disputes with a focus on understanding rather than assigning blame creates a more collaborative space for resolution. By actively listening to all sides and acknowledging the emotions involved, I can identify common ground and facilitate constructive dialogue. This approach not only resolves the immediate issue but also strengthens the trust and mutual respect needed to prevent future conflicts. Building empathy into leadership is a continuous process of learning and self-reflection. It starts with humility, recognising that as a leader, I don't have all the answers and that each team member's perspective adds value. For me, it has meant setting aside preconceived notions and seeking to understand the unique experiences and viewpoints that shape each individual. This openness has not only made me a better leader but has also enriched my understanding of the diverse talents and strengths within my team. Empathy isn't just about understanding challenges; it's also about celebrating triumphs. I make it a point to acknowledge the hard work and achievements of my team members in meaningful ways, whether through a heartfelt conversation or public recognition. This practice reinforces their sense of value and belonging, creating an environment where people feel motivated to give their best. Empathy allows me to see the person behind the performance, recognising the effort and dedication that contribute to success. Practising empathy takes deliberate effort and patience, especially in a high-pressure logistics setting where time is often limited.

I've learned that even brief moments of genuine connection can have a significant impact. Whether it's a casual check-in or a focused one-on-one conversation, these interactions build rapport and show my team that I care about more than just the bottom line. Empathy also means being attuned to non-verbal cues, such as body language and tone, which often reveal more than words alone. Empathy has redefined what leadership means to me. It's not just about driving results or meeting objectives; it's about fostering a culture of mutual respect, trust, and collaboration. Empathy has taught me that leadership is not a one-size-fits-all approach, it's a dynamic relationship built on understanding and compassion. By making empathy a pillar of my leadership, I've been able to create a supportive and engaged environment where team members feel empowered to thrive. Empathy isn't just a skill; it's the foundation upon which meaningful and impactful leadership is built. Communication is the bridge that connects leadership with team members, and emotional intelligence is the foundation that makes it effective. In my leadership journey, I've learned that what we say matters, but how we say it matters even more. Active listening is at the core of meaningful communication. For me, this means not just hearing words but understanding the emotions and intentions behind them. When team members feel truly heard, they are more likely to trust and open-up. Non-verbal communication also plays a vital role. Facial expressions, tone of voice, and body language can convey empathy and understanding far more effectively than words alone. Being mindful of these cues has strengthened my ability to connect with my team. Transparency fosters trust. I've found that being honest and open, even when delivering difficult news, builds respect and credibility. Leaders who communicate with integrity create an environment where team members feel secure and valued. Encouraging open dialogue is essential. By creating a safe space where team members can share their thoughts, I've witnessed incredible ideas and solutions emerge. Communication that connects isn't one-sided; it's collaborative. Clarity in communication eliminates confusion and aligns efforts.

I've learned to express expectations clearly and check for understanding, ensuring that everyone is on the same page and working towards a common goal. Communication that connects is intentional, empathetic, and dynamic. It's not just about exchanging information but about building relationships. When leaders communicate with emotional intelligence, they inspire loyalty, foster collaboration, and create a culture of mutual respect. Communication is more than the exchange of words; it's the heartbeat of leadership, shaping the way connections are built, and goals are achieved. In my journey, I've discovered that effective communication is rooted in emotional intelligence, enabling me to engage not just with words but with understanding and intention. It's about creating a bridge that connects ideas, aligns efforts, and fosters trust. Every conversation, whether routine or challenging, has the potential to strengthen bonds and inspire confidence. Through clear and thoughtful communication, leaders can transform interactions into opportunities for growth and collaboration. Active listening has become a cornerstone of my approach to communication. It's not enough to hear the words; the emotions, intentions, and context behind them are equally important. I've found that when team members feel genuinely listened to, they are more inclined to open up, share ideas, and trust the leadership process. Active listening requires focus and patience, allowing me to pick up on nuances that might otherwise go unnoticed. By being fully present, I not only gain a deeper understanding of my team but also demonstrate respect and validation, which are crucial for building strong relationships. Non-verbal cues often speak louder than words. I've learned to pay attention to body language, facial expressions, and tone of voice, as these elements often reveal what isn't being said outright. A supportive nod, a warm tone, or maintaining eye contact can communicate empathy and understanding far more effectively than words alone. Being mindful of my own non-verbal signals is equally important. How I carry myself, the expressions I wear, and even the pauses I take can all influence how my message is received. This awareness has deepened my ability to connect with my team on a more meaningful level. Transparency is a critical element of communication that connects. I've seen how honesty and openness, even in the face of difficult news, can build credibility and trust. Sharing the "why" behind decisions, admitting mistakes, or being upfront about challenges creates a culture of respect and security. Transparency doesn't mean sharing everything indiscriminately but being intentional about what and how information is conveyed. When team members feel included in the process, they are more likely to buy into the vision and work towards common goals with confidence. Creating a safe environment for open dialogue has been transformative in my leadership experience. Encouraging team members to share their ideas, concerns, and perspectives without fear of judgement unlocks creativity and innovation. I've witnessed remarkable solutions emerge when individuals felt empowered to speak up. This kind of openness fosters collaboration and reinforces the idea that every voice matters. As a leader, it's my responsibility to set the tone for these conversations, ensuring that all contributions are valued and that differences are embraced as strengths. Clarity in communication is essential for avoiding misunderstandings and aligning efforts. I've learned the importance of expressing expectations clearly, breaking down complex information into manageable parts, and confirming understanding to ensure everyone is on the same page. Clear communication extends to feedback as well. Providing constructive, actionable guidance delivered with empathy helps team members grow and feel supported. This clarity doesn't just drive performance; it builds a sense of purpose and direction, motivating individuals to excel. Communication that connects is an intentional, empathetic, and dynamic process. It's about building relationships, not just disseminating information. When leaders communicate with emotional intelligence, they foster an environment of mutual respect, collaboration, and trust. I've seen how thoughtful communication inspires loyalty and strengthens the fabric of a team, creating a culture where everyone feels valued and motivated. Leadership through connected communication isn't just effective; it's transformative, turning ordinary interactions into moments of meaningful impact. Emotional intelligence is the cornerstone of great leadership, and throughout this chapter, we've explored how its five pillars come together to transform the way leaders connect with their teams. It's not just about knowing the right strategies or achieving results; it's about creating a culture where relationships are prioritized, where people feel understood, supported, and inspired. As a leader, I've learned that emotional intelligence enables us to go beyond transactional leadership to create environments of trust, collaboration, and shared success. The journey toward becoming an emotionally intelligent leader isn't an easy one, but it is deeply rewarding. Through self-awareness, I've gained a better understanding of myself, what drives me, what challenges me, and how my emotions impact those around me. This awareness has allowed me to lead with purpose and intention, rather than being swept away by the demands of the moment. With self-regulation, I've learned to pause and reflect, turning moments of frustration or tension into opportunities for thoughtful and constructive action. These are skills that have transformed my leadership, providing a steady hand for my team to rely on, even in the most difficult of times. Motivation, as I've come to realize, is more than a drive to reach goals. It's about igniting that same fire in others, helping them see the bigger picture and empowering them to give their best. Leadership is not just about achieving success but about fostering a sense of shared purpose. When leaders can inspire their team to aim higher and reach further, it creates an energy that propels everyone forward. This kind of leadership fuels long-term success, as it instills a culture where people are motivated not just by the need for results, but by their desire to contribute to something greater than themselves. At the heart of emotional intelligence lies empathy, which has completely reshaped my approach to leadership. It's through empathy that I've learned to connect with my team on a deeper level, to understand their struggles, challenges, and goals.

This has allowed me to build bridges between team members, turning conflict into collaboration and fostering a culture of mutual respect and understanding. Empathy has not only helped me navigate difficult situations but has allowed me to celebrate the successes of my team in ways that make each individual feel valued. The ability to communicate with clarity, honesty, and intention is a vital part of emotional intelligence. In my leadership journey, I've learned that communication isn't just about what's being said, but how it's being heard. Creating an open, honest dialogue within the team builds trust and encourages transparency. When leaders communicate effectively, they foster an environment where ideas are shared freely, conflicts are resolved constructively, and everyone feels empowered to contribute. Communication is the bridge that links leadership with the heart of the team, and it's where true collaboration begins. Emotional intelligence isn't a destination, it's a continual journey of growth and learning. It requires intentional effort, self-reflection, and a deep commitment to understanding both oneself and others. For me, it's been a process of becoming more attuned to the emotional dynamics within my team and adjusting my leadership style to meet the needs of each individual. The results of this journey have been transformative. It has not only made me a more effective leader but also a more compassionate and empathetic person. At its core, emotional intelligence is about creating an environment where everyone can thrive. It's about leading with both the mind and the heart, empowering others to step into their potential and contribute meaningfully to the collective success. The true power of leadership lies in the ability to inspire trust, collaboration, and shared purpose. Emotional intelligence humanizes leadership, turning a team into a unified force with a common vision. When we lead with emotional intelligence, we don't just achieve goals, we create a legacy of growth, connection, and lasting impact.

TIMOTHY K ELLSWORTH

WALKING THE TALK
Inspiring Excellence

Leadership is not just about words, it's about actions that speak louder than anything that can be said. Early in my journey, I quickly came to understand that what I do matters far more than what I say. As a leader, the expectations I set, the values I promote, and the culture I foster are all shaped by my behaviour, not just by the messages I communicate. I've found that the way I act on a daily basis speaks volumes to my team, guiding their responses and shaping their approach to work. Leading by example isn't a one-time effort or a strategy to deploy in certain situations; it's a continuous commitment to embody the principles I expect from my team. One of the most powerful lessons I've learned is that authenticity is at the heart of leadership. When I lead with integrity, humility, and genuine care for those around me, it resonates deeply with my team. I've learned that authenticity builds trust, and trust is the foundation of a high-performing, cohesive team. Team members won't fully buy into a vision or mission if they don't believe the leader is fully committed to it themselves. The commitment to authenticity has meant that I've needed to align my actions with my words at all times, understanding that the consistency between the two forms the bedrock of leadership. Consistency is another critical factor in leading by example. It's not enough to display the values I cherish occasionally; I must live them day in and day out. I've learned that my actions are constantly under observation, and it's the small, consistent choices I make that shape the culture of my team. Whether it's showing up on time, treating others with respect, or being transparent in tough situations, my behaviour sets a precedent. When I consistently uphold the standards I set, I reinforce the importance of those standards for the team. Humility plays a key role in walking the talk. A leader who is willing to admit their mistakes, seek feedback, and embrace their own areas for growth sets a powerful example for the team. This humility fosters a culture where team members feel safe to make mistakes, learn, and improve without fear of judgment. Actions have a ripple effect. As a leader, I've come to appreciate how the energy and attitudes I bring into a room can have an immediate impact on the mood and morale of my team. When I show commitment, positivity, and a willingness to push through challenges, I've found that these behaviours are often mirrored by my team members. The ripple effect of leading by example spreads throughout the team, creating a shared sense of purpose and determination. It's not just the big, visible actions that matter but also the small, everyday decisions that accumulate to form a strong, unified culture. Walking the talk means translating the values we talk about into actionable behaviours. I've learned that a leader's credibility comes from aligning their actions with their words. When I'm consistent in demonstrating the qualities I expect from others, whether it's perseverance, empathy, or accountability, I show my team that these values are not just theoretical ideals but practical realities that can be lived out in our work every day. I've seen firsthand how when I lead by example, I not only earn the respect of my team but also inspire them to take ownership of the shared goals and to approach challenges with the same mindset. Walking the talk is the foundation of true leadership. It's not just about telling others what to do, it's about showing them what's possible by embodying the values that drive us forward. Leadership is about setting the stage for success by creating an environment where everyone feels supported, empowered, and aligned with the mission. When I lead with actions that reflect the highest standards, I create a culture that thrives on mutual respect, trust, and commitment. This culture becomes the heart of our success, where every team member feels connected to the vision and motivated to contribute their best work. Walking the talk isn't just a strategy, it's the very essence of leadership. The commitment to values is what drives the culture of any organization, and I've learned that as a leader, my actions are the foundation of this commitment. Over time, I've come to understand that when leaders actively demonstrate their core values, they provide a clear and compelling blueprint for the entire team to follow. For me, leading by example means ensuring that respect, integrity, and collaboration aren't just words spoken in meetings, but principles actively integrated into the way we operate daily. Living the values of an organization goes beyond just mentioning them, it means embedding them in every decision, big or small. When I make decisions, I do so with respect, integrity, and a commitment to fairness at the forefront of my mind. These values serve as a compass, guiding the choices I make and the way I interact with others. When my decisions reflect these core principles, I notice that they not only inspire my team but also reinforce the importance of making values-based decisions in their own work. It creates a culture where every member of the team knows that their actions should align with the same principles that guide leadership. When I prioritize values like transparency, respect, and collaboration, the entire team gravitates toward these ideals. I've learned that values-driven leadership fosters a shared sense of purpose, a feeling that we're all pulling in the same direction. It transforms an organization from a collection of individuals into a united team, working towards a common goal. I've seen how this alignment improves the cohesiveness of the group, making it easier to navigate challenges, find solutions, and celebrate successes together. However, living out these values is not always easy. Tough situations inevitably arise, and they test our commitment to the principles we hold dear. During challenging times, I've found that staying true to my values is essential, not just for me as a leader, but for the team as a whole. When adversity strikes, it's easy to be tempted by shortcuts or to make decisions that go against the values we hold. But I've learned that it's in these moments, when things aren't going as planned, that staying grounded in our core values demonstrates true resilience.

It's through this steadfast commitment that I've been able to lead by example, showing my team that doing the right thing is often the hardest but always the most rewarding path. Upholding values also means fostering accountability within the team. I've found that when I hold myself to the highest standards, it encourages my team to do the same. It's not enough for a leader to talk about values; they must embody them at all times, even when no one is watching. When I demonstrate integrity, fairness, and accountability in my actions, it sends a powerful message to the team. It shows them that there are no exceptions to the principles that guide us, and that we're all responsible for upholding them. This mutual accountability creates a culture of trust, where everyone is invested in ensuring the team's success. Values-driven leadership is not a one-time effort or a box to check off; it's a continuous practice. I've learned that leading with values requires mindfulness, dedication, and a constant commitment to personal growth. It's easy to lose sight of our core principles when we're caught up in the daily grind, but I've found that regularly reflecting on my values and actions helps me stay grounded. Each day presents new opportunities to reinforce the values that define our team, whether it's through a small gesture or a significant decision. For me, this ongoing commitment to values is what ensures that I remain consistent in my leadership, providing a stable foundation for my team to rely on. My commitment to living out our organization's values is not just about guiding my actions but shaping the collective behaviour of the entire team. When I demonstrate respect, integrity, and collaboration, I set the tone for how we operate as a group. This commitment drives our success, not only by helping us navigate challenges but also by creating an environment where every team member feels empowered to make decisions based on the same principles. Living our values is a powerful tool for building a culture where trust, accountability, and collaboration thrive, and where success is not just measured by results but by the way we achieve them. Leadership sets the tone for accountability, and I've learned that it all starts with me. As a leader, my actions, decisions, and behaviour serve as a model for the rest of the team. Accountability isn't just about enforcing rules, it's about setting an example. When my team sees me own my mistakes, take responsibility for my actions, and consistently follow through on my commitments, it signals that no one is above the standards we collectively uphold. This transparency encourages an open, honest, and supportive environment where everyone understands that accountability is not a choice, but a core value we all embrace. Admitting mistakes is often one of the hardest things for a leader to do, but I've found it to be one of the most important aspects of accountability. Owning up to my errors, whether they're big or small, creates a culture of trust and vulnerability. When I take responsibility for my actions, it sends a clear message to the team that it's okay to make mistakes, as long as we own them and learn from them. I've seen how this transparency strengthens relationships and creates an atmosphere where everyone feels empowered to take risks, knowing that mistakes are part of the learning process, not something to be feared or hidden. Accountability is about follow-through, and I've learned that leaders who consistently meet their commitments build trust and credibility. When I set a goal or make a promise, I understand that it's my responsibility to deliver. I can't expect my team to follow through if I don't. This reliability creates clarity, ensuring that everyone knows what to expect from me and what I expect from them. It's in these moments, when I meet or exceed my commitments, that I reinforce the idea that accountability is a two-way street. It's not just about checking off tasks, it's about building a culture where people can count on each other to do what they say they will do. One of the most powerful things I've learned about accountability is that it's contagious. Accountability isn't a top-down mandate, it's a shared responsibility. When I show that I'm willing to be held accountable, others are more likely to follow suit. I've seen this ripple effect in action, when a leader sets a high bar for themselves, team members rise to meet it. Accountability becomes embedded in the team's culture, where everyone takes ownership of their actions and decisions, knowing that their individual contributions matter to the success of the whole. Setting clear expectations is essential in fostering accountability. I've learned that one of the best ways to ensure everyone takes ownership of their work is to communicate roles, responsibilities, and goals explicitly. When expectations are clearly outlined, there's no room for confusion or misunderstanding. I take care to make sure my team knows exactly what is expected of them, both in terms of performance and behaviour. This clarity eliminates ambiguity and allows everyone to focus on achieving the team's goals with confidence. By establishing and communicating clear standards, I set the stage for accountability to thrive. Self-assessment is a critical part of my personal accountability. I regularly reflect on my own performance to ensure that I'm aligned with the high standards I expect from my team. This self-reflection helps me stay grounded, identify areas for improvement, and make adjustments when necessary. It's important to recognize that accountability is not a one-time effort; it's an ongoing process. By assessing my own performance, I not only hold myself accountable but also ensure that I continue to grow as a leader. This continuous improvement mindset creates a culture where accountability is not just a goal, but a lifelong journey that everyone embraces. Accountability in leadership is about integrity, not perfection. I've come to understand that accountability isn't about being flawless, it's about being honest and responsible in all that I do. When I demonstrate integrity through my actions, I help create a culture where accountability is valued and practiced by everyone. It's not about getting everything right all the time, but about taking responsibility for both successes and failures and learning from every experience. This culture of accountability empowers the team to take ownership of their work, collaborate more effectively, and ultimately achieve greater success together. Consistency in leadership is fundamental to building trust, and I've learned over time that the best way to lead is through predictable, reliable actions. When my actions align with my words, it sends a clear message to my team that I am someone they can count on. Trust doesn't happen overnight, it's cultivated through consistent, deliberate behaviour. Whether it's a deadline, a promise, or a value I've spoken about, staying consistent in my approach builds that trust over time. One of the most important things I've learned about consistency is that it fosters stability within a team. When my behaviour is steady and my decisions are dependable, my team feels a sense of security. Knowing that I will uphold our values regardless of the circumstances creates a foundation of respect. I've seen how stability in leadership can make all the difference, particularly during periods of uncertainty or change. When things get tough or complicated, it's my consistent behaviour that provides the anchor. It's not just the big decisions, but the everyday small acts of integrity that add up to create a culture of consistency. Inconsistent behaviour, on the other hand, erodes trust. I've witnessed how even a single lapse in judgement or failure to follow through can shake the confidence of a team. If I say one thing but act in a different way, it creates doubt. This doubt undermines trust, and without trust, a team cannot function at its best. That's why I strive to remain steadfast in my commitment to leading by example. I know that I'm not perfect, but I make it a priority to consistently align my actions with the values I expect from my team. If I fall short, I take ownership and correct it, because that consistency in acknowledging imperfections is also part of building trust. Consistency isn't just about the big, strategic decisions I make, it's about the everyday actions that contribute to the overall culture of the team. I've realized that leadership is built on the small moments, the ones where my actions speak louder than words. From being punctual for meetings to treating everyone with respect, these seemingly small behaviours add up to create a larger impact. When I show up on time, when I follow through with promises, when I show kindness and fairness, I am demonstrating consistency. These actions remind my team that I care about them, that they can count on me, and that we are all working towards a shared goal. Leading with consistency also means staying true to our core mission and values, especially during times of change. Change can create disruption, and it's easy to lose sight of what matters most when navigating through uncertainty. However, I've found that reinforcing our core values during transitions provides a sense of continuity. When I continue to uphold our mission and stay grounded in what we believe, it provides my team with a stabilizing force. It allows us to move forward with confidence, even when the path ahead is unclear. Consistency in these moments keeps us focused, reminding us of who we are and what we're working to achieve. Consistency in leadership is also about building credibility. I've learned that when I consistently demonstrate fairness, transparency, and respect, my credibility grows, and with it, the team's trust in me. It's the everyday actions that establish my reputation. My team will begin to mirror the behaviours they see in me, creating a cycle of trust and respect that strengthens our collective culture. In leadership, credibility isn't a one-time achievement, it's something that's earned and reinforced over time through consistent actions. In leadership, consistency isn't optional, it's essential. It's the thread that weaves integrity, trust, and respect into the fabric of a thriving culture. I've come to understand that consistency in my behaviour doesn't just benefit the team, it strengthens the organization as a whole. When I lead with consistency, I create an environment where team members feel valued, supported, and confident in their roles. It helps build a culture where everyone is committed to doing their best, because they know that I will always be there, showing up, acting with integrity, and guiding the team toward success. Consistency is the cornerstone of leadership, and when I uphold it, I contribute to a culture where trust and respect are not just ideals, but daily practices. Inspiration in leadership is not just about motivating words, it's about the power of action. Over time, I've learned that my team is far more inspired by what I do than by what I say. Living out my values through consistent actions sends a much stronger message than any speech or directive could. When I demonstrate the principles I expect from others, whether it's taking on additional work during peak times or stepping up to support a colleague, it shows my team that I am just as committed as they are. This level of dedication encourages them to mirror these behaviours, creating a culture where everyone is motivated to give their best. For me, leading by example requires intentionality. Inspiration doesn't happen by accident; it takes conscious effort. When I go above and beyond to show my commitment, my actions send a powerful signal. Whether it's staying late to ensure a deadline is met or being the first to volunteer for tough tasks, it's these small but meaningful actions that inspire my team. I've noticed that when I show up with enthusiasm and a willingness to do the hard work, it sparks a sense of shared responsibility in the team. They feel encouraged to match my energy and effort, creating a collective spirit of excellence. Authenticity is at the core of inspiring leadership. I've found that when I lead with sincerity and passion, it resonates deeply with my team. Authenticity doesn't just amplify inspiration, it also fosters trust. When my team sees that I am genuinely invested in the work, in their growth, and in our shared mission, it builds a connection that words alone could never achieve. I don't just talk about values; I live them. Whether it's showing empathy, being transparent, or consistently displaying integrity, my authenticity encourages my team to do the same. The more real I am in my leadership, the more my team responds with the same level of engagement and dedication. Inspirational leadership requires perseverance, especially in the face of adversity. I've learned that when challenges arise, it's crucial to stay focused and optimistic. When things get tough, I don't just manage the situation, I also model the behaviour I want to see. Staying calm, maintaining a positive outlook, and actively problem-solving shows my team that obstacles can be overcome. Through my actions, I help them see that challenges aren't roadblocks, but opportunities for growth. By demonstrating resilience and determination, I teach my team how to approach adversity with the same resolve. Acknowledging wins, both large and small, is another key to inspirational leadership. I've discovered that celebrating successes as a team, not just individually, reinforces the idea that we all contribute to the overall success. When I take the time to recognize outstanding contributions, it not only boosts morale but also inspires others to strive for excellence. It's not about simply patting someone on the back, it's about genuinely appreciating their effort and making them feel valued. This recognition fuels motivation and fosters a sense of shared accomplishment that drives the entire team forward. Inspiring others is also about empowering them to take ownership and grow. I've seen first-hand how encouraging my team to step into leadership roles, make decisions, and take responsibility for their work builds confidence and competence. As they see their own abilities grow, their motivation increases. Empowering others doesn't just lighten the load, it creates a ripple effect where team members encourage each other and strive for collective success. When I support my team in their development, I not only inspire them to be better leaders but also strengthen the team as a whole. Leading through action is about igniting potential. By consistently living out the values I want to see in my team, I create an environment that fuels inspiration and motivation. When I show my team what's possible through my own efforts, it sparks their desire to do the same. The energy and commitment I bring to my role aren't just about achieving goals, they are about inspiring the people around me to believe in themselves and the team. When actions speak louder than words, leadership becomes a dynamic force that shapes both individuals and the collective spirit, driving us all towards success. Visibility in leadership is about more than just showing up, it's about being genuinely engaged and present for the team. When a leader makes themselves available, it sends a strong message that they care deeply about the well-being and success of those they lead. It's not about hovering over every detail or micromanaging, but about being approachable, involved, and accessible. The more present a leader is, the more the team feels supported and empowered. This engagement fosters connection, trust, and respect, as team members see their leader actively participating and showing interest in their work. This level of visibility makes the team feel validated and motivated to give their best performance. A leader's presence during critical moments speaks volumes, and this is something that truly matters. During times of crisis or major challenges, the team needs to know their leader is there to navigate the situation with them. It's easy to be a leader when things are running smoothly, but leadership is truly tested in adversity. Being present, calm, and focused during tough times shows the team that obstacles can be overcome together. This visible commitment to being there during every situation helps to build loyalty and trust. When a leader stands firm in the face of challenges, it provides the team with the confidence to persevere and succeed. It's this level of engagement that drives the team to strive for excellence, knowing they are supported not just in their work but also in their personal development. When a leader creates a positive and energised atmosphere, it motivates the team to push forward, even during times of stress or uncertainty. Visibility in leadership also brings with it accountability. A leader's actions and how they carry themselves are constantly being observed by the team. This visibility reinforces the importance of leading by example. When a leader is transparent about their mistakes and takes responsibility, it encourages the team to do the same. It shows that no one is exempt from accountability, and that high standards apply to everyone. When a leader holds themselves to the same expectations they have for the team, it strengthens mutual trust and fosters a sense of unity. Accountability is key in creating a culture where everyone understands they contribute to the success of the team. Being visible as a leader isn't just about showing up physically; it's about being present emotionally and mentally as well. Leadership is more than just making decisions or offering guidance, it's about creating a culture of connection. By showing up with an open mind and heart, a leader can build deeper relationships with the team. This emotional presence signals that the leader is invested in the success and well-being of the team. It creates an environment where people feel safe to express themselves, ask for help, and take risks. When a team knows their leader is genuinely there for them, they are more likely to give their best efforts and trust the direction the team is heading. Visible leadership fosters a culture of support, connection, and trust. It's about showing up in every sense of the word, demonstrating commitment to the team's success, not just through words but through actions. When a leader is actively engaged, communicates transparently, and holds themselves accountable, it creates a sense of unity and shared purpose within the team. Visibility as a leader is not just about being seen, it's about being truly present and supportive. This approach lays the foundation for a culture where everyone feels valued, heard, and motivated to contribute to the collective success of the team. Leading by example is the heartbeat of a thriving culture, and it's the foundation upon which great teams are built. Throughout this chapter, we have examined how the actions of a leader directly influence the trust, accountability, and excellence within their team. From living out core values to maintaining consistency, every action plays a crucial role in shaping the culture. Leadership is about actively modelling the behaviours that promote the organization's success. When leaders walk the talk and demonstrate the values they expect from their team, it fosters an environment of mutual respect and accountability. The ripple effect of a leader's actions extends throughout the team, creating a culture where every member feels valued, supported, and motivated to do their best work. The impact of leading by example has a long-lasting impact, setting the stage for sustained success and growth. Consistency in leadership builds the trust necessary for any team to function at its best. It creates a culture where team members feel secure, knowing that their leader will always uphold the values that guide their work. Inspiring through visible leadership adds another layer of strength to the culture. By being engaged, approachable, and present during both challenges and triumphs, a leader becomes a pillar of support for the team. Visible leadership fosters unity and resilience, a leader who actively communicates and involves the team in decision-making empowers everyone to feel connected to the mission, driving collective success. The true measure of leadership is not found in titles or positions, but in the actions that inspire others to follow suit. Leading by example is about being the change we want to see in the world. When leaders embody the values, they champion, they set a powerful example for others to follow. By doing so, they create a legacy of excellence and unity, where every team member is motivated to contribute their best and empowered to thrive. This unified approach fosters an environment where individuals feel both accountable and encouraged, knowing that their efforts are not only valued but integral to the team's success. Each person becomes a vital piece of the larger puzzle, contributing to a culture where collaboration thrives, and personal growth is supported. Through thoughtful leadership, consistent communication, and shared values, team members are inspired to push past limitations and continuously seek improvement. Empowered with the right tools, mentorship, and a clear vision, they develop a deeper sense of ownership over their work and the goals of the team. Together, through our actions, we can build a culture that fuels success, nurtures creativity, and helps every team member reach their full potential. This shared commitment ensures that success is not just an individual achievement, but a collective one, a victory built on a foundation of respect, collaboration, and dedication, where every team member can proudly contribute to a legacy of greatness that will echo for years to come.

TIMOTHY K ELLSWORTH

CULTURE KILLERS
Hidden Saboteurs

As a leader, mentor and coach, I've seen the detrimental effects of punishing an entire team for the missteps of a few individuals. While it may seem like an efficient way to enforce standards or send a message, this approach often backfires. Imagine being a high-performing team member who consistently goes above and beyond, only to be lumped in with those who fail to meet expectations. It's demoralizing and unfair. Instead of fostering accountability, this tactic alienates the very people who are driving your team's success. The reality is blanket punishments undermine the principle of fairness. Fairness is a cornerstone of any strong workplace culture, and when it is perceived to be absent, trust erodes quickly. Team members start to feel that their individual contributions do not matter because they are judged collectively. This creates an emotional disconnect, making team members less likely to take pride in their work or invest in the team's goals. When fairness is sacrificed, so is engagement. Over time, this approach can breed apathy. When team members realise that their efforts won't be individually recognised or rewarded, they may begin to adopt a "why bother" attitude. After all, if hard work is met with the same consequences as poor performance, what incentive is there to go the extra mile? This apathy doesn't just affect the individuals who feel slighted, it spreads like a virus through the team. High performers may leave, seeking environments where their contributions are valued, leaving behind a demotivated team struggling to maintain momentum. Punishing the entire team for the actions of a few also fosters resentment, not just toward management but toward the underperformers themselves. Instead of addressing the root of the issue, this method pits team members against one another. High achievers may begin to feel hostility toward their peers who are dragging them down, creating a toxic dynamic within the group. The result is a fractured team that struggles to collaborate effectively, let alone achieve excellence. One of the most concerning outcomes of this approach is the loss of trust in leadership. I've observed how quickly trust can disintegrate when team members feel management is unwilling to tackle issues head-on. When leaders take the easy way out by punishing everyone instead of addressing individual accountability, they send the message that they either lack the courage to confront problems or do not value their team's unique contributions. Trust is difficult to rebuild once it's broken, and a culture without trust is destined to falter. To truly address the issue, leaders must commit to tackling problems at their source. This means having the tough conversations with those who are not meeting expectations and providing them with the tools and support they need to improve. It's not about pointing fingers or shaming individuals but about holding them accountable in a way that is constructive and respectful. This not only resolves the issue at hand but also demonstrates to the rest of the team that their efforts are recognised and valued. Leadership isn't about taking the path of least resistance; it's about fostering a culture where fairness, accountability, and respect are non-negotiable. By dealing directly with those responsible for underperformance, you reinforce the idea that everyone's contributions matter and that excellence is achievable when the team operates as a cohesive unit. As a mentor and coach, I can assure you that the investment of time and effort in individual accountability pays dividends in morale, trust, and productivity. A one-size-fits-all punishment may seem convenient, but in the long run, it fits no one. I have seen firsthand how cancelling team events in response to unmet standards can do more harm than good. On the surface, it may seem like an effective way to incentivise improvement, but the message it sends is deeply problematic. When leaders take away events designed to celebrate and connect the team, it signals that the value placed on the team's effort is conditional, tied only to perfection. This approach can feel punitive and heavy-handed, eroding the morale that those very events are meant to build. Team events are not merely perks or luxuries; they are essential to fostering connection and camaraderie. These gatherings provide a unique opportunity for colleagues to step outside their usual roles and interact as people, not just as professionals. They build trust, strengthen bonds, and remind everyone of the bigger picture. By cancelling these events, leaders strip away one of the most effective tools for creating a positive and collaborative culture. The result is a team that feels disconnected and demoralised, not motivated to improve. One of the most troubling aspects of this approach is that it punishes everyone, including high performers and those striving to meet standards. Imagine being a dedicated team member who consistently delivers results, only to have a long-anticipated event cancelled because of the actions of others. It's disheartening and frustrating. This blanket punishment approach sow's division, as team members begin to resent not only leadership but also their peers whose shortcomings led to the decision. This resentment can create rifts within the team that are difficult to mend. Cancelling events as a disciplinary measure also undermines the principle of trust. Team members begin to feel that management is more interested in controlling behaviour than in supporting the team's growth and well-being. This perception fosters an environment of fear and compliance rather than one of mutual respect and collaboration. In the long term, this damages the team's engagement and their faith in leadership, making it harder to rally them around future goals. Rather than resorting to the drastic measure of cancelling events, leaders should view these moments as opportunities to engage with their team and address challenges collaboratively. Use the time together to celebrate small wins, acknowledge hard work, and openly discuss the obstacles preventing the team from meeting standards. This approach not only preserves morale but also creates a sense of shared accountability, where everyone feels invested in the team's success. When mentoring a new leader to remember that recognition and celebration are not rewards to be earned but vital elements of a thriving workplace culture. By maintaining these traditions even in challenging times, leaders send a powerful message: that they value their team as people, not just as producers. This doesn't mean ignoring underperformance, but it does mean addressing those issues directly and constructively without taking away what binds the team together. Leadership requires balancing accountability with encouragement. Cancelling events may seem like a shortcut to enforcing standards, but it comes at the cost of connection, trust, and morale. Instead, focus on using events as a platform to inspire, connect, and recharge the team while addressing any performance issues through transparent communication and targeted support. As a mentor coach, I can attest that preserving these moments of joy and unity strengthens not only the team's culture but also their ability to rise to challenges together. The fun freeze may feel like a quick fix, but it often leaves everyone out in the cold. Recognising national holidays, alongside the diverse cultural holidays represented within your workplace, is more than a nice gesture; it's a fundamental part of fostering inclusion and complying with human rights legislation. I've seen how workplaces thrive when they respect and celebrate the cultural and national identities of their team members. Failing to acknowledge these significant days doesn't just risk alienating team members, it can also put organisations at odds with the principles of Equity and inclusion outlined in human rights frameworks. Human rights legislation emphasises the importance of creating workplaces free from discrimination, where everyone feels respected and valued. Acknowledging national holidays, as well as the cultural holidays that reflect the diversity of your team, is a tangible way to uphold these principles. By recognising and celebrating these occasions, leaders demonstrate their commitment to inclusion and ensure that no one feels overlooked or excluded based on their background. This isn't just about compliance; it's about creating a workplace culture where everyone feels they belong. Failing to honour national holidays, while recognising others, can unintentionally send a message of imbalance. Team members might feel their cultural identity is less valued, leading to resentment and disengagement. When an organisation prioritises inclusivity, it makes a conscious effort to celebrate all relevant holidays, from national observances to culturally significant days, ensuring every team member feels respected and included. This approach strengthens workplace bonds and affirms the organisation's commitment to equitable treatment. Recognising all holidays represented in your workplace embodies the very definition of inclusion. It moves beyond tokenism, demonstrating an authentic respect for the diverse experiences and identities within your team. As a mentor coach, I stress that inclusivity is about more than intentions, it's about visible actions that affirm every team member's value. By celebrating national and cultural holidays, leaders actively contribute to a sense of shared identity while embracing the richness of diversity. Additionally, acknowledging these holidays provides an opportunity for education and connection. Teams can learn about one another's traditions and histories, fostering understanding and empathy. This not only strengthens interpersonal relationships but also helps build a culture of collaboration and mutual respect. When leaders embrace these moments to bring their teams together, they create an atmosphere where inclusion is felt, not just spoken about. Human rights legislation sets the foundation, but it's up to leaders to go beyond compliance and actively promote inclusivity. Recognising holidays is a simple yet powerful way to align with these values. It demonstrates an understanding that people's identities and traditions matter. The workplace becomes more than a space for productivity, it becomes a community that celebrates its members in meaningful ways. I've seen how taking these steps transforms workplace culture. When team members feel seen, respected, and included, their engagement and morale soar. They take pride in their work because they know they are valued not just for their output but for who they are. Acknowledging all holidays, whether national or cultural, isn't just about compliance or goodwill, it's a cornerstone of creating a thriving, inclusive workplace. Allowing poor behaviour or performance to go unchecked is one of the quickest ways to erode a positive workplace culture. When team members observe that underperformers face no Consequences, it sends an unmistakable message: mediocrity is acceptable. This perception undermines trust in leadership and creates resentment among those who consistently go above and beyond. Over time, high performers may begin to feel demoralised, questioning the value of their efforts when others are not held to the same standards. Discipline, when applied constructively and consistently, is the backbone of a culture of accountability. It is not about punishment but about maintaining clear expectations and ensuring everyone adheres to them. When leadership fails to address poor behaviour, it signals that the rules are flexible and that individuals are free to disregard them without Consequence. This not only weakens the integrity of the workplace but also creates a chaotic environment where no one feels secure in what is expected. A lack of accountability leads to the gradual erosion of workplace standards. When poor performance becomes normalised, the ripple effects can be seen across the team. Team members who once gave their best effort may begin to pull back, feeling their contributions are undervalued in an environment that rewards complacency. This degradation of standards affects productivity, quality, and even customer satisfaction, as the collective effort of the team suffers from the absence of accountability. Leadership that fails to enforce discipline risks losing the respect of the team. Team members want to see that managers are willing to act, when necessary, especially to uphold fairness and protect the team's integrity. A reluctance to address issues may be interpreted as weakness or indifference, leading to a breakdown in trust. Without trust, team cohesion unravels, and team members become less engaged in their work, knowing that their leaders are not invested in maintaining a high-performing and respectful environment. The effects of unchecked poor performance are not confined to the individuals directly involved. The broader team dynamic is also affected as resentment grows among team members who must carry the extra weight left by underperforming colleagues. This imbalance creates tension and frustration, which can escalate into conflicts and reduce the sense of unity within the team. When accountability is lacking, team members may become divided, focusing more on perceived injustices than on collaboration and shared goals. Constructive discipline is the solution to preventing these issues. Addressing poor performance or behaviour directly and fairly shows team members that leadership is committed to maintaining standards. Effective discipline involves setting clear expectations, providing actionable feedback, and giving individuals the opportunity to improve. When team members see that accountability is applied fairly, they are more likely to respect leadership decisions and feel motivated to meet or exceed the expectations set for them. A culture of accountability fosters trust, fairness, and a sense of shared purpose within the team. Team members who know they will be recognised for their efforts and held responsible for their shortcomings are more likely to remain engaged and committed. Discipline, when handled thoughtfully, reinforces the idea that everyone's contributions matter and that no one's poor performance will be allowed to diminish the achievements of the team. In the absence of accountability, the culture deteriorates, but with it, the workplace thrives. Micromanagement may seem like a way to maintain control, but it often causes far more harm than good. When leaders feel the need to oversee every detail, it conveys a clear message: "I don't trust you to do this on your own." This lack of confidence can deeply undermine morale, leaving team members feeling undervalued and second-guessed. Instead of fostering a culture of growth and empowerment, micromanagement creates an environment where fear of making mistakes takes precedence over innovation and initiative. Over time, micromanagement fosters a sense of dependency among team members. Team members begin to wait for instructions rather than taking the initiative to solve problems or contribute new ideas. This dependency not only stifles creativity but also slows down processes, as team members become hesitant to act without explicit approval. A once-dynamic team can quickly devolve into a group of individuals simply going through the motions, reluctant to step out of line for fear of criticism or correction. The ripple effects of micromanagement extend beyond the individuals being managed. It creates a bottleneck in productivity as decisions are delayed, waiting for managerial approval. This approach also places an unnecessary burden on leaders, who spend their time monitoring and controlling tasks rather than focusing on strategic goals and big-picture thinking. The result is a workplace where both leaders and team members feel drained, overworked, and disconnected from the broader mission of the organisation. Micromanagement also discourages team members from developing their skills and taking ownership of their roles. When leaders continually step in to handle tasks or correct details, team members miss out on valuable opportunities to learn and grow. This lack of autonomy prevents team members from building confidence in their abilities, leaving them less prepared to tackle challenges independently. A workplace culture that prioritises empowerment over control allows individuals to flourish, but micromanagement robs them of that chance. The emotional toll of micromanagement cannot be overlooked. Team members subjected to this style of leadership often feel demoralised and unmotivated, as their contributions are overshadowed by constant oversight. This can lead to increased stress, burnout, and even turnover, as team members seek workplaces where their abilities are trusted and valued. Leaders who embrace a more hands-off approach, offering support and guidance rather than control, are far more likely to retain talented and engaged team members. An empowered team is one where individuals are trusted to make decisions and take responsibility for their work. Leaders who resist the urge to micromanage and instead focus on providing clear expectations, regular feedback, and the resources needed for success create a culture of accountability and innovation. When team members are given the freedom to experiment, take risks, and learn from their mistakes, they develop a sense of ownership that drives engagement and results. Breaking the cycle of micromanagement starts with self-awareness and a willingness to let go of unnecessary control. Leaders must recognise that their role is to guide and support rather than to oversee every detail. Trusting team members to rise to the challenge not only builds a stronger, more capable team but also allows leaders to focus on higher-level objectives. When autonomy and trust are prioritised, teams become more innovative, resilient, and aligned with the organisation's vision, creating a workplace culture where both team members and leaders can thrive. Failing to recognise and celebrate achievements in the workplace creates an invisible barrier to morale and engagement. When team members feel that their hard work and dedication go unnoticed, it leaves them questioning their value to the team. This sense of invisibility can lead to disengagement, where the passion for contributing diminishes because there's no acknowledgment of the effort. A lack of recognition not only dampens spirits but also quietly fosters dissatisfaction, making it harder to retain talented individuals. Recognition is one of the simplest yet most powerful tools for fostering a motivated and engaged workforce. It doesn't need to come in the form of grand gestures or expensive rewards. A heartfelt thank-you, a public acknowledgment of a job well done, or a small token of appreciation can make a world of difference. When these moments are neglected, it sends a damaging message that team members' contributions, no matter how significant, are not valued. The absence of recognition has a cumulative effect, chipping away at the foundation of a strong workplace culture. Over time, team members may begin to mirror the indifference they perceive, performing only to meet the bare minimum required. Without the positive reinforcement of recognition, the behaviours and achievements that drive excellence may fade into the background. This erosion of motivation eventually impacts the team's overall productivity and morale, creating an environment where mediocrity becomes the norm. Recognition is more than just a "nice-to-have"; it's a critical component of team member engagement and retention. Acknowledging successes helps build confidence and a sense of purpose. It reinforces positive behaviours and encourages team members to push boundaries and exceed expectations. When leaders consistently fail to provide this feedback, they miss opportunities to strengthen their teams and align their efforts with organisational goals. Overlooking achievements also damages trust between leaders and their teams. Team members who consistently deliver results may feel overlooked or underappreciated, which can create resentment. When team members perceive that their contributions are ignored, it undermines their belief that the organisation values their efforts. This erosion of trust can lead to high turnover rates, as team members seek environments where their work is acknowledged and respected. A culture of recognition promotes unity and collaboration. Celebrating individual and team achievements fosters a sense of pride and shared purpose. Team members are inspired to continue striving for excellence when they see their efforts publicly appreciated. Recognition strengthens relationships within teams, as colleagues become more aware of and supportive of each other's contributions. This collective spirit creates a resilient culture where both individual and organisational goals are met with enthusiasm. Prioritising recognition is not just about making team members feel good, it's about sustaining a thriving workplace. Leaders who actively and consistently acknowledge accomplishments demonstrate that they value the people who drive the organisation's success. This practice fuels engagement, boosts morale, and encourages continuous improvement. A workplace culture where achievements are celebrated is one where team members feel seen, respected, and motivated to bring their best to the table every day. Few things can damage a team's cohesion and trust as quickly as a lack of clear communication. When team members are left in the dark about decisions, changes, or expectations, uncertainty takes root. Without reliable information, people often fill the gaps with assumptions that are rarely positive. This creates a culture of doubt and insecurity, where rumours thrive, and confidence in leadership begins to falter. Open and transparent communication is the backbone of trust within any organisation. Team members need to understand the "why" behind decisions, the "what" of their roles, and the "how" of achieving collective goals. When leaders fail to share this information, it leaves teams directionless and fragmented. I have seen how this communication breakdown can cause even high-performing teams to lose their momentum and sense of purpose. A communication blackout isn't just about missed memos or updates; it reflects a deeper failure to value team members as partners in the organisation's success. People want to feel involved and informed, not treated as mere cogs in a machine. When information is withheld, it conveys a message that their input and understanding are not important. Over time, this leads to disengagement, as team members feel disconnected from the organisation's vision and their role within it. In my own experience, I have witnessed how providing timely, honest communication can transform a struggling team. Clear communication doesn't mean sugar-coating challenges or avoiding difficult conversations. On the contrary, it's about fostering a culture where people know they can trust what they hear from their leaders, even when the news isn't what they hoped for. Trust grows when teams feel their leaders are upfront and invested in their collective success. The absence of communication also creates inefficiencies that ripple through an organisation. Without a shared understanding of goals and expectations, team members waste time and energy heading in different directions. This lack of alignment not only diminishes productivity but also frustrates team members who want to contribute meaningfully. Clear communication eliminates ambiguity, helping teams focus their efforts and work toward shared objectives. When leaders communicate openly, they foster a sense of unity and shared responsibility. Team members are more likely to buy into decisions and changes when they understand the rationale behind them. This buy-in is critical for navigating transitions and overcoming challenges. Open communication also encourages feedback, creating a two-way street where team members feel heard and valued. The result is a workplace where collaboration and trust become the norm. Maintaining consistent and open communication takes effort, but the rewards are undeniable. Leaders who prioritize transparency demonstrate respect for their teams and a commitment to their success. They understand that communication isn't just about sharing information; it's about building relationships and fostering a culture of trust. By keeping teams informed and engaged, organisations lay the foundation for long-term success, where everyone feels like a vital part of the journey. Favouritism is one of the quickest ways to erode trust and harmony within a team. When some team members are consistently given preferential treatment, it sends a clear message that not everyone is valued Equally. This can manifest in countless ways, such as assigning high-profile projects to the same individuals, offering privileges unavailable to others, or turning a blind eye to mistakes from those in the "inner circle." For those left out, the experience can be deeply demoralizing and lead to a sense of alienation. When leaders play favourites, they unintentionally divide the team into "insiders" and "outsiders." This division creates an "us versus them" dynamic that undermines collaboration and teamwork. Instead of fostering a sense of shared purpose, the team becomes fractured, with members focused on navigating unfair treatment rather than working together toward common goals. The long-term damage to morale is often difficult to repair, as trust in leadership is significantly diminished. As someone who has observed the impact of favouritism in different settings, I've seen how it can poison even the most promising teams. Talented individuals who feel overlooked or undervalued often become disengaged, withdrawing their effort and creativity. When hard work and dedication don't lead to opportunities or recognition, team members begin to question the fairness of the system. This disengagement doesn't just harm individual performance; it lowers the overall standard of excellence. Favouritism also sends the wrong message about what a workplace values. Instead of highlighting merit, effort, or results, it places personal preferences above professionalism. This practice diminishes respect for leadership, as team members perceive decisions to be based on bias rather than fairness. Over time, it fosters a toxic environment where cynicism and frustration replace trust and enthusiasm. The effects of favouritism don't stop with morale; they ripple outward, impacting productivity and innovation. When opportunities and resources are unfairly distributed, some team members lose the motivation to excel, while others may avoid collaboration out of resentment. This leads to inefficiencies, missed opportunities, and a team culture where potential is wasted. Favouritism isn't just a morale killer; it's a barrier to achieving excellence. It's crucial for leaders to recognize that fairness is the cornerstone of a thriving workplace culture. Every team member deserves the opportunity to contribute, grow, and succeed based on their abilities and efforts. Transparency in decision-making and a commitment to impartiality are essential for fostering trust. By consistently treating everyone with respect and fairness, leaders create an environment where people feel valued and motivated to bring their best. To build a culture of excellence, favouritism must be eliminated in favour of a merit-based approach. Leaders should strive to evaluate contributions objectively, ensuring that rewards, opportunities, and recognition are distributed fairly. This not only boosts morale but also reinforces a culture where effort and achievement are celebrated. When team members see that fairness guides decisions, they are inspired to collaborate and excel, knowing that their work will be valued and rewarded. Allowing toxic behaviours to linger unchecked is like introducing a slow-acting poison to a team's culture. When negativity, gossip, or disrespect are tolerated, they create an environment where distrust and dissatisfaction thrive. Team members quickly notice when such behaviours are overlooked, and it sends an unspoken message that these attitudes are acceptable. The result is a ripple effect that can undermine morale and cohesion. Toxicity doesn't just harm those directly involved; it impacts everyone in its radius. Team members who strive for positivity and collaboration often feel frustrated and powerless in the face of unchecked negativity. Over time, these individuals may disengage, opting to keep their heads down rather than confront an environment that feels hostile or draining. This withdrawal can lead to a decline in team performance and a loss of valuable contributions. Negativity, when left unaddressed, tends to spread like wildfire. A single individual with a toxic attitude can influence others, creating a culture where complaints, gossip, and disrespect become the norm. In such an environment, trust erodes, collaboration suffers, and the team's focus shifts from achieving goals to navigating conflict. This type of dysfunction can quickly derail even the most talented groups. I have seen first-hand how addressing toxic behaviours directly and decisively can transform a struggling team. It isn't easy to confront these issues, especially when the toxic individual is a high performer or a longstanding team member. However, ignoring the problem only exacerbates it. By stepping in, leaders can send a powerful message that no one is above the standards of respect and professionalism. A culture of excellence demands more than just technical skill; it Requires emotional intelligence and mutual respect. When team members know that toxic behaviours will not be tolerated, they feel safer and more empowered to contribute. This sense of security fosters open communication, innovation, and collaboration, creating an environment where everyone can thrive. Addressing toxicity isn't about creating a punitive culture but about setting clear expectations and holding everyone accountable. Leaders must lead by example, modelling the behaviours they want to see in their teams. Open communication, consistent feedback, and a commitment to fairness are crucial tools for maintaining a positive workplace environment. When leaders show that they take toxicity seriously, they inspire their teams to do the same. The cost of tolerating toxic attitudes far outweighs the challenges of addressing them. By prioritising a culture of respect and positivity, organisations can protect their teams from the damaging effects of negativity. A healthy, supportive workplace isn't just good for morale; it's essential for achieving sustained excellence. When every team member feels valued, respected, and heard, they are more motivated to work together towards shared success. When an organisation fails to define or uphold its core values, it leaves team members navigating a culture without a compass. Core values are not just lofty ideals; they are the bedrock of a thriving workplace. Without them, confusion takes root, and team members are left guessing at what the organisation stands for and how they should align their actions with its purpose. This uncertainty breeds frustration, mistrust, and a sense of disconnection from the broader mission. Core values provide clarity and consistency. They set the standard for how decisions are made, how challenges are addressed, and how people interact. When leaders neglect to clearly define these values, it creates a leadership vacuum. Without this foundation, team members often create their own interpretations of what is acceptable, leading to fragmented behaviours and conflicting priorities. Over time, the lack of alignment becomes a drain on morale and productivity. The danger does not end with a failure to define values; inconsistent application is just as damaging. When some team members are held accountable to one set of standards while others are allowed to deviate, fairness is undermined. This inconsistency leads to mistrust in leadership and a perception that the organisation is hypocritical. A team member who sees values applied selectively will struggle to take them seriously, and the shared cultural foundation begins to crumble. Without strong values, the organisation struggles to create a sense of purpose. Vision and purpose are what unite a team, giving them something larger than themselves to work toward. When values are absent or inconsistently upheld, team members can feel as if their work is disconnected from any meaningful goal. This disconnect breeds disengagement, as people question the importance of their contributions and their place in the team. Upholding core values requires more than words, it demands intentional action. Leadership must model the behaviours that reflect these values, creating an environment where principles are seen in action every day. I have witnessed how transformational it is when leaders not only state their values but embody them. It signals to the team that these values are not just corporate slogans but the heartbeat of the organisation. Strong values also foster resilience. In times of crisis or uncertainty, a clear and upheld set of principles provides a guide for decision-making and action. Core values give the organisation stability, allowing team members to navigate challenges with confidence. They create trust, as team members can rely on the fact that decisions will be grounded in a shared understanding of what matters most. This trust is the glue that holds teams together when times are tough. A unified culture flourishes when core values are clear, consistently upheld, and embraced by all. Team members feel grounded and aligned, knowing their work contributes to a meaningful vision. This alignment not only enhances engagement but also inspires a sense of pride and belonging. A workplace grounded in core values becomes more than just a place to work, it becomes a community united by a shared commitment to excellence. Throughout this chapter, we've explored the pitfalls that can destroy a thriving workplace culture. Punishing the team for the mistakes of a few, cancelling morale-boosting events, neglecting to recognise achievements, playing favourites, tolerating toxic behaviours, and failing to communicate or uphold core values all erode trust and create disengagement. We've seen how these actions foster confusion, resentment, and a sense of disconnection among team members. When left unchecked, they lead to a fragmented and unmotivated workforce, ultimately derailing the organisation's mission and goals. To counter these culture killers, leaders must embrace emotional intelligence, trust, and relationship-building as the cornerstones of their approach. Emotional intelligence allows leaders to understand the impact of their actions on the team, respond empathetically, and foster an environment where people feel valued. Trust, built through honesty and integrity, is essential for creating a culture where team members feel safe to take risks, innovate, and give their best effort. Without trust, even the most well-intentioned strategies fall flat. Relationships form the backbone of any team, and strong relationships are forged through consistent, authentic interactions. Leaders who prioritise getting to know their team members as individuals, understanding their strengths, challenges, and aspirations, build loyalty and engagement. Honesty and integrity ensure that team members feel they are part of an organisation that stands for something meaningful. When leaders model these values, they inspire the same behaviour in their teams. Creating a culture of excellence requires daily reinforcement. Just as negative behaviours can take root without intervention, positive behaviours need consistent reminders to thrive. By sharing daily messages of positivity and clear expectations for behaviour, leaders embed the values they want to see reflected throughout the team. Celebrating small victories, addressing challenges constructively, and reiterating shared goals remind everyone of the culture they are building together. A positive workplace culture is not built overnight, it is the result of deliberate and ongoing effort. It is shaped by every decision, every interaction, and every moment of accountability. Leaders who invest in their team's emotional well-being, build trust, and lead with integrity cultivate a culture that resonates deeply with team members. This culture becomes a force for motivation, driving the team toward success and creating an environment where excellence is not just expected but celebrated. The power to shape a culture lies in consistent, thoughtful leadership. By fostering connection, demonstrating fairness, and upholding clear values, leaders can transform their teams into cohesive, motivated, and inspired groups. When culture is nurtured and protected, it becomes the driving force behind innovation, collaboration, and sustained success. A thriving culture does not just act as a support system; it becomes the bedrock upon which the team's greatest achievements are built. It encourages risk-taking and experimentation, knowing that failure is not a setback but an opportunity for growth. In this environment, creativity flourishes, as team members feel empowered to think outside the box and share their ideas without fear of judgment. Moreover, a strong culture fosters a deep sense of trust, making collaboration seamless and effective. With everyone aligned on core values and objectives, communication becomes more open, conflicts are resolved more efficiently, and collective effort becomes a driving force toward shared goals. Make the choice to build a culture that uplifts and empowers, and you will see the extraordinary potential of your team unleashed. This commitment to cultivating a healthy culture transforms how your team operates, motivates individuals to bring their best selves to work each day, and strengthens the bonds that connect everyone to the team's mission. Over time, these collective contributions create not only individual success but organizational excellence, unlocking new opportunities, establishing a competitive advantage, and creating a work environment where innovation and collaboration are limitless. By prioritizing culture, you are not just fostering a team but igniting a movement where the potential of each individual is magnified, and success is inevitable.

CONCLUSION

As we bring this exploration of building and sustaining a thriving team culture to a close, it is essential to reflect on the journey we have undertaken. The essence of a successful team lies not just in reaching goals but in how those goals are achieved, through unity, trust, transparency, collaboration, and recognition. A team that excels is one where each member feels a deep connection to the collective mission and understands the value of their contributions. This sense of belonging and purpose is what transforms ordinary teams into extraordinary ones, capable of overcoming challenges and achieving lasting success. Creating and maintaining a family-like culture within your team is not a one-time effort but an ongoing commitment. It requires continuous nurturing, adaptability, and reinforcement to ensure that the culture evolves alongside the team. Leaders play a crucial role in this process, modeling the behaviours they wish to see and consistently reinforcing the values that underpin the team's success. However, sustaining this culture is a shared responsibility, with every team member contributing to the environment in which they work. By recognizing and appreciating each other's efforts, fostering open communication, and prioritizing collaboration over competition, the team can grow stronger, more cohesive, and more resilient over time. As you move forward, remember that the power of a strong team lies not only in its accomplishments but in the way those accomplishments are achieved. The journey from values to victory, from cultivating connections to celebrating triumphs, is one that requires dedication, patience, and a shared commitment to excellence. By investing in your team's culture, you are not just driving short-term success but laying the foundation for sustained growth and achievement. This investment cultivates an environment where every team member feels valued, supported, and empowered to contribute their best, knowing that their work plays a pivotal role in the greater mission. As trust, collaboration, and shared values guide your collective efforts, success becomes inevitable, not as a mere outcome, but as a reflection of the strength and unity within your team. The dedication to building a strong culture goes far beyond achieving immediate goals; it sets the stage for continuous improvement, innovation, and resilience in the face of challenges. Together, as one united force, your team can continue to thrive, innovate, and make a lasting impact on your organization and beyond. The power of a deeply rooted culture transcends external successes, it becomes an unshakable foundation from which each individual and every group endeavor, can rise to unimaginable heights. When your team is empowered by a shared vision, no obstacle is too great, no opportunity too distant. You are not simply shaping a culture for today but leaving a legacy for future generations, where your team will continue to inspire, lead, and transform, perpetuating a cycle of success for years to come.

The potential is endless, and the future is yours to create. The question now is not whether your team will succeed, but how far they can go when empowered by a culture that inspires excellence in every moment.

www.ingramcontent.com/pod-product-compliance
Lightning Source LLC
Chambersburg PA
CBHW071057240526
45471CB00016B/1987